Praise for Brian Doyle's *Credo*

"Brian Doyle's subjects in these vivid essays and compact narratives and historical parables are faith, family, and friendship, and he brings to them a robust sensitivity and an edgy lilt. In an age when discussions of religious and personal matters too often verge on the sentimental and the mawkish, Doyle handles issues of meaning and belief with disarming humor and deft honesty. In *Credo* we witness an encounter between timeless questions and an utterly modern man, a man whose desires and sorrows, whose temptations and hopes are shared by us all."

Cullen Murphy, managing editor, *The Atlantic Monthly*

"Brian Doyle has a gift for words. In *Credo* he uses this gift to give new meaning to many common practices that we take for granted, like the sign of the cross. His simple accounts of practices breathes new life into these acts of faith. I was often inspired while reading this simple but profound book. You will be, too."

Theodore M. Hesburgh, CSC,
president emeritus, University of Notre Dame

"Brian Doyle writes beautifully about faith, a subject most modern writers are afraid of. These essays are skillful, scholarly, passionate, lively, and – above all – brave."

Ian Frazier, author, *Great Plains*

"Brian Doyle's writing – filled with the velvet and lightning of daily life, deftly told – will make you drop your sorrow and follow. This is a religion of devoted attention, pain embraced, and great good humor. I read to learn with him: whence this warm wisdom and boyish verve? Somewhere this writer learned how to be honest about the good. Part ethnography of the electric friction of Catholic life, part hymn to ordinary miracles, this book will sing in your hands like prayer."

Kim Stafford, director, Northwest Writing Institute

"Religion is as ancient as the stars and as mysterious as the Maker. It is also as simple as a child's giggle and as practical as a peanut butter sandwich. Out of all of faith's many elements, from the transcendent to the everyday, Brian Doyle weaves a vision for a complete and modern spiritual life. At a time when the world is most in need of soul, this is something to be very thankful for."

H. Emerson Blake, managing editor, *Orion*

"Brian Doyle's grace-full essays open windows on a world of light, even for those outside his faith."

Donald S. Lamm, editor and publisher

"There is a furnace burning inside Brian Doyle. It's fueled by grace and love and a lyrical imagination. Doyle's fire is beautifully manifest in these writings. *Credo* is the kind of book that will stay with you. It is memorable in its intelligence and heartwarming in its wisdom."

Barbara Ras, author, *Bite Every Sorrow*

"Washed by the rain, blessed by geese and family, and always, always surprised, Brian Doyle richly describes a species of peace we all might aspire to reach. In wonderful stories that teeter between a belly laugh and a broken heart, he lets us know that for him, faith is fit company for nothing less than the complete human parade. Humble, sound, and shimmering with hope and question, Brian Doyle's book of belief is a wonder."

Robert Michael Pyle, author, *Wintergreen* and *Chasing Monarchs*

CREDO

CREDO

Essays on grace, altar boys, bees, kneeling, saints, the Mass, priests, strong women, epiphanies, a wake, and the haunting thin energetic dusty figure of Jesus the Christ

by
Brian Doyle

Saint Mary's Press
Christian Brothers Publications
Winona, Minnesota

Where these essays first appeared:

America: "Notes from a Wake"
The American Scholar: "Altar Boy"
Ar Mhuin na Muice: "A Note About Saint Finbar"
Boston College Magazine: "Name-Calling"
The Catholic Sentinel: "A Note on Epiphanies," "Have You Anything
   Here to Eat?" "Massing," "Washed Clean," "A Saint for Hard-
   working Women"
Commonweal: "From *The Diary of Saint Kevin of Glendalough,*"
   "A Sunday, in October, Under a Flight of Geese"
Companions: "Christ's Elbows"
Liguori: "As Strong As the Very Ribs of the Earth"
Notre Dame Magazine: "Grace Notes" (in different form)
Portland Magazine: "A Thin Ragged Man," "In the Country of
   Poetry," "Last Supper"
U.S. Catholic: "Glory Bee," "A Note on the Death of the *Index
   Librorum Prohibitorum,*" "Credo," "Father, Son, Spirit Holy,"
   "The Announciation," "A Note on Kneeling"

The quotes on page 120 are from *The Blue Jay's Dance: A Birth Year,*
by Louise Erdrich (New York: HarperCollins, 1995), pages 70–72.
Copyright © 1995 by Louise Erdrich.

The publishing team included Michael Wilt, development editor;
Rebecca Fairbank, copy editor; James H. Gurley, production editor;
Cindi Ramm, cover designer; pre-press, printing, and binding by
the graphics division of Saint Mary's Press.

Cover painting by Laure Heinz; author photo by Joanie Digan

Printed in the United States of America

Printing: 9 8 7 6 5 4 3 2 1

Year: 2007 06 05 04 03 02 01 00 99

ISBN 0-88489-622-6

to Lily, Joseph, and Liam,

go mbeannai Dia thu,

God keep you forever.

❖

Acknowledgments

Most of the essays in this volume first saw light in a startling number and variety of journals, and the Author bows in the directions of those publications' editors, men and women of obvious discernment.

My gratitude, then, to Joseph Epstein, Thomas McGrath, Margaret O'Brien Steinfels, Michael Patrick Mulcrone, Robert Pfohman, Ben Birnbaum, Fr. George Hunt, Deb Shannon, Patrick Jordan, Kerry Temple, and Walt Collins.

To Fr. David Tyson, and Messrs. Tony DiSpigno and John Soisson, who have allowed the University of Portland's *Portland Magazine* to be as substantive and creative as it is, sincere thanks.

To Ethel and Jim Doyle, who hatched the Author, showed him a clean and gentle manner of living, and have blessed him for forty-two years with their courage and love, heartfelt thanks.

To my parents' able assistant tutors in the nuances of family life – my sister, Elizabeth Marie, and my brothers, Kevin, Peter, and Thomas – grinning thanks. For my late brother, Seamus, prayers.

And to Mary Miller Doyle, for her astonishing grace and humor and character, as strong as bone, awed thanks.

Contents

Preface

Credo, Latin for "I believe," which I do, very strongly, in a number of things.

I believe that there is a mysterious and graceful and miraculous Coherence stitched through this world.

I believe that this life is an extraordinary gift, a blink of bright light between vast darknesses.

I believe that the fingerprints of the Maker are everywhere: children, hawks, water.

I believe that even sadness and tragedy and evil are part of that Mind we cannot comprehend but only thank; a Mind especially to be thanked, oddly, when it is most inscrutable.

I believe that children are hilarious and brilliant mammals.

I believe that everything is a prayer.

I believe that my wife is the strongest and most graceful female being I have ever met, with the possible exception of my mother.

I believe that a family is a peculiar and powerful corporation, lurching toward light, webbed by love, a whole ridiculously bigger than its parts.

I believe, additionally, that friends are family.

I believe, deeply and relievedly, in giggling.

I believe that the best of all possible breakfasts is a peanut butter-and-cheddar-cheese sandwich with a cup of ferocious coffee, taken near the ocean, rather later in the morning than earlier, preferably in the company of a small sleepy child still in her or his rumpled and warm pajamas, her or his skin as warm and tawny as a cougar pelt.

I believe that love is our greatest and hardest work.

This book is a labor of love; love is all I ever write about; and I hope that you will not only enjoy it as an experience but find something of use or delight in these pages, and not overmuch to snort at.

My personal thanks to you for reading it. I suspect we will never meet, but we are connected by these sentences, begun in my home and finding a sort of home in you and yours, and this connecting is much more powerful than we know.

Brian Doyle
Portland, Oregon

Altar Boy

I will go up to the altar of God
  The giver of youth and happiness.
                              Psalm 43

Introit

I missed one Mass as an altar boy – the Tuesday dawn
patrol, 6:00 a.m., Father Dennis Whelan presiding. He was
a good-natured fellow, a cigar smoker even though he was
a little young for it, that kind of guy, but he was furious
when I trudged back to the sacristy after sitting through
the second half of Mass in the very last pew.

Where were you?

I was late, Father.

You miss another and you're out of the corps.

I'm very sorry, Father.

It's no joke to be all alone out there.

Yes, Father.

I knew why he was peeved; I was the key to his famous
twenty-two-minute Mass. He pulled off this miracle week
after week, without ever looking at his watch. His Mass
drew the faithful by the dozens, especially businessmen
trying to catch the weekday 6:30 train into New York City.
One time Whelan had the 6:00 on Saint Patrick's Day, and

we had nearly fifty people in the church – still a record for our parish, I bet.

Working with Whelan was a pleasure; he was a real artist, someone who would have made his mark in any field. He had all the tools – good hands, nimble feet, a sense of drama, a healthy ego, the unnerving itch to be loved that all great performers have. He did not rush his movements, mumble, or edit his work. He was *efficient,* yes – he'd send his right hand out for the chalice as his left was carving a blessing in the air, that sort of thing – but every motion was cleanly executed and held in the air for the proper instant, and he had astounding footwork for such a slab of meat. He was one or two inches over six feet tall, 250 pounds maybe, big belly sliding around in his shirt, but he was deft on the altar and could turn on a dime in the thick red carpet. He cut a memorable double pivot around the corners of the altar table on his way to his spot, and he cut that sucker as cleanly as a professional skater before a Russian judge.

My job was simple: I was the wizard's boy, and the whole essence of being a great altar boy was to be where you needed to be without seeming to get there. Great altar boys flowed to their spots, osmosed from place to place. They just appeared suddenly at the priest's elbow and then slid away infinitesimally like Cheshire cats. There were other arts – quick work with the hands, proper bell ringing, a firm hand with matches and candles, the ability to project a sort of blue-collar holiness on the stage, that sort of thing – but the flowing around like a five-foot-tall column of water was the main thing, and it was damned hard to learn. Rookies spent their whole first year, and often two, lurching around the altar like zombies, a tick behind Father's moves, which led to, horror of horrors, an irritated Father gesturing distractedly for what he needed. Extra gestures from the wizard were the greatest sins, and we recoiled in horror when we saw them when we were at Mass with our families and out of uniform. At such moments, when the clod on the altar forgot to ring the bells, or brought the wrong cruet, or knelt there like a stone when he should have been liquiding around the altar in a flutter of surplice sleeves, I closed my eyes in shame and in memory, for my rookie year was a litany of errors too long to list, and my graduation from rookie to veteran was a source of great pride to me.

Gloria

Whelan was all business out there from the moment he strode purposefully through the little doorway from the sacristy. He had to duck a bit to get under the lintel easily, but even this little dip was done smoothly and powerfully, as if he had trained for it. This quick duck-and-rise move made it appear that he was leaping onto the stage, and he always startled the rail birds getting in a last ask before the lights went up; by the time Whelan was front and center, the old birds were back in their pews doing the rosary ramble.

Whelan ran his Mass like clockwork, and God help the boy who was still sleepy, because the man knew our marks like they were chalked on the floor, and he expected us to be quick with the equipment of the Mass – glassware, towels, smoke. Cruets were to be filled to the neck, incense respectfully removed from the boat and properly lit in the thurible, hand towel clean and folded over the left arm, Mass book open to the right page, bells rung sharply at exactly the instant he paused for the sharp ringing of the bells. He also liked his wine cut with water in advance, half and half. Most priests liked to mix it themselves during Mass. Some drank mostly water with only a touch of wine for color and legitimacy; some drank the wine straight, with barely a drop of water. Few priests drank a full load of wine; even the heavy hitters found cheap burgundy distasteful at dawn. We did, too, although there were more than a few boys who drank wine in the musty stockroom, and every altar boy at some point gobbled a handful of Communion wafers to see how they tasted fresh from the box. They tasted like typing paper. After I discovered that the hosts came wholesale from a convent in New Jersey, the consecrated Host never tasted quite as savory again.

Oremus

I joined the altar boys because my older brother was in the corps and because my parents expected it. Also you could get out of class for funerals. Funerals didn't pay anything, but weddings did, usually a buck, although there were rumors of five-dollar weddings, and it was said of one boy that he had once received a twenty-dollar bill from a bride's father who was drunk. Baptisms didn't pay – a quarter, maybe, if you were doing twins. The way to make money was to do funerals and to work the banks of candles on either side of the altar. The big ones were on the left and the little ones were on the right – "big ones for the horses and little ones for the dogs," as Mr. Torrens, the altar master, said with an enigmatic smile. He was a horseplayer, I think.

People would come up to the candles before and after Mass, and if you were there in uniform they'd hand you the money, even though the steel box was right in front of them. Large candles were a dollar, and small ones were a quarter.

Light a big one for my grandmother, they'd say, crumpling a bill into your hand.

Here's a quarter for my boy at sea.

Here's a quarter for a marriage.

A quarter for the Pope's health.

Two smalls, for my intentions.

A dollar for the dead.

The code among us was that coins placed in your hand were yours; bills went into the box. The theory was that we were just standing there and the women (they were mostly women) were handing us money out of the goodness of their hearts. This was the first tickle of sin for some of us, and while the practice enriched some boys, it was by no means universal, partly because our cassocks had no pockets and partly because Mr. Torrens learned about it from a first-year boy and after that kept a sharp eye on us from the sacristy door. A boy named Frank Rizzo was asked to leave the corps because of this and it caused great embarrassment to his family. He became a bully in adolescence and probably still is.

The Poem of the Twenty-two Rites and Thirteen Masses

When I was an altar boy there were twenty-two rites for the Mass, and we were expected to know them even though we were to be witnesses and assistants at only one, the Roman rite, by far the world and Olympic champion in Western civilization, but there were actually two other Western rites and a startling total of nineteen Eastern Catholic rites. All twenty-two rites remain in my mind not unlike a poem, and so I chant the Poem of the Twenty-two Rites, which I dedicate to Father Dennis Whelan, wherever he may be: Abyssinian, Albanian, Ambrosian, Armenian, Bulgarian, Chaldean, Coptic, Georgian, Greek, Hungarian, Italo-Albanian, Malabar, Malankar, Maronite, Melkite, Mozarabic, Roman, Rumanian, Russian, Ruthenian, Serbian, and Syrian. I even remember that the Ambrosian rite was used only in Milan, and the Mozarabic rite only in Toledo and Salamanca in Spain. And then there are the thirteen Masses within the Roman rite: the *Missa Cantata,* or sung Mass (or "High Mass") sung by a priest and a choir, the Gregorian Masses (a series celebrated for thirty consecutive days for the release of a soul in purgatory), the Low (the "usual Mass," like the ones I assisted Father Whelan with), the Pontifical (said by a bishop), the Solemn (sung by a priest with acolytes, choir, deacon, and subdeacon), the Votive (priest's choice of intentions), *Missa Pro Populo* (said by pastors by Church law eighty-eight times a year), Mass of a Saint, Mass of Exposition, Mass of Reposition, Mass of the Catechumens (the first half of Mass, before the big moment), Mass of the Faithful (second half), and Mass of the Presanctified (part of the Good Friday Mass during the Passion of Christ).

To remember all this, is that prayer or foolishness?

Mass of the Faithful

After Father Whelan was on his mark, facing the congregation from behind the altar, Mass was underway. The pieces of it snicked into place like oiled parts of an engine. Opening prayers, prayer for the intention of the day, Gospel, Eucharist, serving of Eucharist along the rail, left to right and back again, cleanup and closing prayers, back to the front of the altar for the brisk procession back into the sacristy. Or, in the order of the Latin prayers we learned and then unlearned, *aufer a nobis, oramus te, Kyrie* (Greek, left over from the first and second centuries a.d. before the Mass went Latin), *Gloria, Alleluia, Credo, Dominus Vobiscum, Oremus, Sanctus, Te igitur, Communicantes, Hanc igitur, Quam oblationem, unde et memores, Supra quae, Supplices, per quem, per ipsum, Pater Noster, Libera nos, Agnus Dei, Domine, Ite missa es, placeat,* and then a rush for the door, or, in the case of the priest and the altar boy, a dignified retreat to the sacristy.

As Whelan ducked back under the sacristy lintel, he was a different man, and even before he was across the room you could see the steel go out of his body. At the counter he took off his alb and hung up his rope belt on the inside of his closet door. Then he peeled his surplice off over his head like a boy yanking off a sweater, and then he sat down on his stool and lit a cigar. By then my surplice and cassock were hanging in my locker and I was sitting in one of the two chairs by the door. It was considered bad form to leave the sacristy before Father left. Some boys waited impatiently by the door, but I rather liked Whelan and enjoyed the postmortem:

Good job out there, son.

Thank you, Father.

Could do the bells a little sharper.

Yes, Father.

Then still them with your off hand.

Yes, Father.

Are we on next week?

Monday for me, Father.

Ah, that'll be Father Driscoll.

Driscoll was another brisk guy, although not quite so smooth as Whelan. He was a good deal younger, and he lingered over the prayers a little. It was said that he had a hair shirt and the stigmata, and we watched his hands closely when he carved the prayers during Mass. You couldn't really tell about the stigmata; there were marks there, but he could have cut himself working in the priests' garden, which was the domain of a little Italian Jesuit who made pickles and such. Driscoll's small hands were always moist, and he had the unusual habit of shaking hands with his altar boys after a Mass; he did this as part of his disrobing ritual, and he would actually come into our little locker room to shake hands if we'd forgotten about it. He always seemed out of place there, and he didn't stay any longer than the handshake.

Once a visiting Franciscan who didn't know the custom wandered into our locker room after a Sunday Mass and sat down companionably. There were four of us boys there at the time, two just finished and two suiting up, and I remember the uncomfortable silences after the priest's friendly questions; we weren't used to a priest in our room, and he was an oddity anyway, with his hooded brown robe and bare feet in enormous sandals. He had gnarled feet like the roots of oak trees. The veins on his feet looked like cables and his toenails were as big as quarters. He finally realized the score and left, after shaking our hands. His hands were a lot bigger and drier than Father Driscoll's. He didn't have the stigmata.

Years later I realized with a start that Christ probably looked a good deal like the Franciscan, with his dusty feet and pocked face, and I had ignored the guy, wished him gone no less than shaky Peter had wished Jesus gone from his past before the cock crew; Peter standing there in the icy darkness, the fire at his feet sparking up into the dangerous night, sharp voices coming at him like needles, he shifts uneasily from foot to foot and damns his friend as easily, as thoughtlessly, as you might crush a beetle; then a shooting pain of light in the sky, dawn crawls over the hills, and right in his ear, as loud and shrill as a scream, comes the shriek of a rooster and the horrible knowledge that *he has betrayed the man he loves.* . . .

Consecration

Actual belief in the miracle was mixed among us boys, although all of us watched the priests' hands with awe at the instant the Host was changed into the living, breathing Body of Christ. We did not expect to actually see change steal over the Host itself, as we had been told ad infinitum by the nuns that the miracle was beyond human ken, but we did half-expect to see a priest's hands burst spontaneously into flame as he handled the distilled essence of the Mind that invented the universe. There was some discussion about what we should do if a hand fire broke out. There were two general camps: the first insisted that the water cruet should be flung at the fire, and the second advised a sprint away from the awful miracle and toward the janitor, who spoke only shards of English but who knew how to deal with fire, locked doors, broken bicycle chains, vomit, heart attacks, dog bites, broken teeth, broken noses, blood, and sobbing first graders who peed their pants because they were too shy to raise their hands and ask Sister if they could go to the bathroom.

I could never turn my eyes away from that key moment, though. It was and is the single most mysterious and bizarre belief of my faith, and it was in many ways the thing that set us apart from all other Christian denominations. In later years I would sit in Congregationalist and Episcopalian and Lutheran services and observe the communions of those faiths, the passing of torn bread among the faithful and the circulating cups of wine, and while these acts seemed friendlier to me, more communal than the shivering magic of the Transubstantiation, they seemed insubstantial too, muted, more like a casual brunch than a heartbreaking Last Supper. I always wanted to like the communions of other faiths, but they seemed pale to me. I suppose being dipped in miracles every day inoculates you against the mundane; or at least it shoots your sense of perspective all to hell. I still expect miracles, and I have seen some: my wife, my daughter coming out of my wife, my twin sons coming out of my wife one after another like a circus act, the bolt of light that shot around the room when my uncle died.

Requiem

Recently I went to Mass in the Cathedral of the Madeleine in Salt Lake City. This edifice, a monument to the staying power of Catholicism in the heart of Mormon country, is the church where my late father-in-law was an altar boy in the 1920s. He was also a student there, as the cathedral once housed a grade school in its nether regions (four Congregation of Holy Cross nuns taught eight grades), but it was the altar itself that I was interested in, and during Mass I deliberately detoured past the immense stone altar and proscenium, thinking of the man who once knelt there, garbed in acolyte's robes, draped in youth, not yet the affable patriarch who would sire six children and build a business and hammer a home out of the Oregon woods and die there suddenly among his pastures and gardens, his breath sliding to a halt as his lungs filled with fluid, his wife holding him in her arms as he slumped helplessly to one side of the bed, the look on his face more confusion than pain, his death a great surprise to him on a lovely April morning, the scents of horses and blackberry trickling in the window.

I don't know what I expected to see there, amid the pomp and circumstance of Mass in this garish old castle. I suppose I was looking for the marks of his knees, or the hovering nugget of his soul. He died before I met him, before I could thank him for his daughter and show him my daughter and sons. I have looked for him in the woods and in the wood of the house he made. I have been closest to him near a small pond that he labored to clear from the woods, but the forest in Oregon is a tenacious thing, and it took the pond back after the man died. It is a mouth filled with water. Weeds have grown over it so that it can no longer talk.

Adolesensuous

Certainly being an altar boy was training for the priesthood, in the way that baseball's little leagues are training grounds for the big leagues. We were encouraged to go on outings with the younger priests, who took us to carnivals and baseball games (always the Mets, never the Yankees) and bowling alleys. The eighth graders made a pilgrimage to the seminary at Garrison, New York, every year; the year I went the school had just opened a vast and gleaming sports center, and a quiver of athletic lust went through me like winter wind when the doors to this Xanadu swung open and revealed an oceanic swimming pool and glittering gymnasium with polished hardwood floors and *glass backboards.* We nearly fainted with desire. The young priest showing off this gem had the wit to remain silent as we gaped at Neverland, and my friends and I spent the rest of the day envisioning ourselves sprinting and spinning and scoring thousands of points on that perfect floor, the stands throbbing with local girls tantalized not only by our patent skill but by the thought that we were tadpole priests – how much more enticing to lure a prospective saint down into the willow trees by the river, and there slip a tongue in his mouth and get his hand on your breast and see if the Catholic Church in the vaguely sanctified person of this gangly zit of a boy was indeed convinced that asceticism was a road to holiness.

Combine this athletic Xanadu with the sweeping view of the Hudson Valley below, and the lush playing fields terracing off into the distance, and the sense that a boy living at a high school fully two hours from home was an independent and mature creature, and you had a potent draw for boys on the lip of puberty; but then we were served mystery meat for lunch, in a dank military-style cafeteria, and shown through the cold moist barracks, where narrow metal cots stretched away for miles, where a thousand boys had pulled the pud in a thousand slate-gray stalls, and they lost us. All the way home Father Driscoll chirped the virtues of the seminary, but we were silent, each boy afraid to be the first to burst the poor man's bubble. He might, after all, bear the stigmata; plus we felt sorry for him. He had once been sentenced to a narrow cot and horse burgers and dismal mornings in a dank gray stall where cockroaches did the fandango through scummy puddles.

We went home to our bright houses with joy.

Catechumens

On mornings when I had the 6:00 Mass I would awake in the woolly dark and leave my brothers snoring like bears and pedal through the empty streets with my fists clenched in my jacket pockets and my collar turned up against the whip of dawn. The church was silent and dark. The only light in it was the tabernacle lamp, and the only sign of human life, the stray Styrofoam coffee cups filled with cigarette butts in the back of the church, the spoor of the Nocturnal Adoration Society, which met once a month to conduct a vigil with the Blessed Sacrament, which reposed inside a monstrance on the altar; teams of men would arrive every hour and replace the team in the church, each team yawning as it passed the other, each exchanging muted greetings, a handshake here and there in the dark air, the men checking their watches and settling down on their knees like old horses waiting for dawn.

There were seven lay societies: the Altar Society (for women), the Blessed Virgin Sodality (for young women), the Holy Name Society (for men), the Legion of Mary, the Mother's Club, the Nocturnal Adoration Society, and the Rosary Society (for women). While my ambition was to someday join my father in the Nocturnal Adoration Society, my admiration was highest for the Altar Society, whose members worked liked bees to keep the church and its accoutrements sparkling. "It was they who undertook the laundering of altar linens, communion cloths and surplices, the polishing of the brass candelabra and altar vases, as well as the disposal of withered flowers, ferns, and pot plants," as the Irish writer Mary Lavin notes in her story "A Voice from the Dead." They were an efficient lot, friendly but brisk, and the Good Lord Himself could not help a boy who got in their way when they were stripping the altar linens; more than once I was shouldered against the cold wall of the sacristy by a brisk Altar Society Woman with an armful of God's laundry, on her way purposefully, moving through the waters of the day like a battleship, to her dank basement laundry room and the magic Maytag thundering away down there like the monstrous engine in a tramp steamer.

Incense

Almost always I was at the church before Father Whelan. I would hear his steps in the courtyard and smell his cigar. He smoked villainous cigars, execrable things that smelled like peat moss and burned fitfully if at all. He was always at them, lighting, relighting, puffing determinedly, moaning with despair at the shoddy plug that hung like a zeppelin between his lips. He got them from the tobacconist in the village, a seedy man with a harelip who gave the priests a break, twenty percent off, probably in exchange for future considerations. I knew the price because I once bought a box for Whelan after Mass; he'd been caught short, and after thrashing his pockets like a man with bees on his pecker, he sat me down in the sacristy.

I need a favor, son.

Yes, Father.

It's unorthodox.

Yes, Father.

I need cigars.

Cigars?

Cigars. A box of them.

Yes, Father.

You'll have to go up to the village. You have a bike.

Yes, Father.

Get a box of panatelas. Here's a fiver.

Yes, Father.

Don't smoke any.

No, Father.

Keep the change.

Yes, Father.

None of these coronas, now.

Yes, Father.

What?

I mean No, Father.

Memento

I remember the dark scent of the church at dawn, the dense purple light, the smells of incense and cigars and dust. I remember the dry shuffling of shoes as communicants shambled toward the Host. I remember the twisted faces of saints in the windows, Veronica's pale hand outstretched with a cloth for the face of Christ, the bulging Popeye forearm of Simon as he supported the collapsing Savior. I remember the groaning organ and the reverberating yowl of an infant being baptized in the nave. I remember the stiff black cloth under which you hid all desire and personality as you prepared to assist at a miracle that you did not and could never understand but which you watched for ravenously, like a hawk after meat. For a time we were expected to wear ties under our cassocks, but eventually this stricture was lifted and we were allowed to wear shirts. No jeans, no sneakers, no sandals — this last despite the gnarled treelike feet of the Franciscans on the altar once a month. You buttoned your cassock from the bottom up, to be sure of symmetry, and then you slipped on the starched white surplice. A simple uniform, black and white, unornamented, memorable.

Credo

I have come, in my middle years, to a passionate belief in a Coherence — a pervasive divineness that I only dimly comprehend and cannot at all articulate. It is a feeling, a sense. I feel it most near my elfin daughter, my newborn sons. Last night I stood over the huddled body of my daughter, asleep in her crib, her hair flowing around her like dark water. She had fallen asleep only minutes before, sobbing herself to sleep after soiling herself and her bedding and her bear. She is very sick and cannot control her bowels, and she is humiliated and frightened by this; she fell asleep in my wife's arms, her sobs muffled in the folds of my wife's deep soft flannel shirt. I stand above her now in the dark. She is curled like a question in the corner of her crib. I place my hands together in an ancient gesture of prayer and humility and begin to weep — for love of this child, in fear of illness, in despair at my helplessness. I make a prayer in the dark. I believe so strongly, so viscerally, in a wisdom and vast joy under the tangled weave of the world, under the tattered blanket of our evil and tragedy and illness and brokenness and sadness and loss, that I cannot speak it, cannot articulate it, but can only hold on to ritual and religion like a drowning man to a sturdy ship.

Benedicamus Domino

"And so the Mass comes to an end, in a whirl of purifications and postscripts that do not seek to impress themselves deeply on the mind; one has not enough capacity left for receiving impressions," wrote the English priest and novelist Ronald Knox. "'And every man went to his own house,' as it says frequently in the Old Testament and once in the New, and that is what we do; we must be alone."

Many a time I was alone, when it was all over, when the rail birds had gone from the rail, when the businessmen were walking briskly to their trains. When the audience was gone, the janitor would whip through the church slamming the kneelers back up and slipping missals and songbooks back into their racks behind each pew. Then he would bow before the altar and slip out a side door toward the school. I would wait for the click of the side door closing and then wander out of the sacristy and sit down in a pew and think and listen and wait for something to happen. The building groaned and creaked, the candles fluttered and sizzled, bees and flies bounced off the windows. In the windows were the saints, red and blue and green and pink, their faces and bodies and fluttering hands outlined in lead. After a few minutes I would walk down the aisle, past the empty pews and kneelers and missals and Stations of the Cross, and push through the massive oak door and into the broad fat light of the new day, dazzled.

t²wo

Credo

Recently a friend asked me why I was Catholic. I mumbled the first few reasons that entered my head – the faith of my family, the enticing power of the story, an increasing belief as I age that divinity indeed infuses all things and that Christ, dead in the dust at age thirty-three, was indeed distilled divinity.

My friend was satisfied and moved the conversation along to other things, but I was not satisfied and so have continued to write down reasons that I am Catholic.

I believe that a carpenter's son named Jesus did indeed crack Time in half, enter this world in the guise of a squalling infant, say his piece, be slaughtered for his pains, and crack Time again on his way home. I have no real basis for this belief, and neither do you. We either believe the man or we do not, and I do, for reasons I know and do not know.

Some of those reasons I can articulate. I was born into a Catholic family, and early learned to love the smoke and poetry and incantation of the Roman rite. My friends were Catholic, and we were as bound by our common faith as we were by our exuberant youth, European forebears, and itchy masculinity. Catholicism was the faith of my Gaelic forebears, whom I greatly respect in absentia. It was the faith of my grandmother, who shriveled and died before my eyes when I was twelve years old, and whose funeral Mass taught me the enormous power of ritual, the skeleton that sustains us when we are weak. And Catholicism was the faith of my alma mater, where I stuttered into manhood, and of three of my professional employers.

But I believe in Christ for muddier reasons. Sometimes I desperately need to lean on a god wiser and gentler than myself. Sometimes I desperately need to believe that when I die I will not be sentenced to Fimbul, the Hell winter, where there is only the cold voice of Nothing, but rather I will be at peace and draped in Light. Sometimes I am nudged toward belief by the incredible persistence and eerie genius of the tale: the encompassing love of a Mother, the wordless strength of the Father, the Lord of All Worlds cast ashore on this one as a mewling child in dirty straw. Sometimes I am moved past reason by the muscular poetry and subtle magic of these stories. Sometimes it is an intuitive *yes* as the light fails and the world is lit from below. And sometimes I simply cast my lot with the sheer bravura of such a patently brazen lie. That a man could die and live again is ridiculous; even a child knows that death is the end.

Or is it?

I do not want to be sure about that. I want to meet my quiet father-in-law, a man I never knew, and thank him for the lovely miracle of his last daughter. I want to meet my brother Jimmy, who died in his carriage on a bright April day in 1947. I want to meet William Blake, Dexter Gordon, Crazy Horse. I want to kiss my grandmother again on her leathery cheek. I would like to see my friend Dennis Green, age twenty-three, who died on a humid highway in Florida while I was writing these words. I would like to meet this fellow Christ, who haunts the edges of my dreams, who flits from tree to tree in the forest through which I make my way. I would like to live forever, and hold my wife and daughter and twin sons in my arms until the end of time, and daily read the immense poem of Death Into Life, and grin at the whirl and swirl of its endless unfolding, until the end of Until.

So I am a Catholic, for many reasons. Sometimes I think I might be also a Buddhist, because that faith is calm and wide, and sometimes I think perhaps I am also a pantheist, because I smell divinity in music, herons, drunkards, flowers. But Catholic is my language, Catholic is the coat I wear, Catholic is the house in which I live.

It is a house that needs cleaning, a house in which savagery and cowardice have thrived, where evil has a room with a view, where foolishness and greed have prominent places at the table. But it is also a house where hope lives, and hope is the greatest of mercies, the most enduring of gifts, the most nutritious of foods. Hope is what we drink from the odd story of the carpenter's odd son. When we eat his body in the ludicrous miracle of the Mass, we hope in him, and with him, forever and ever, world without end, amen, amen, amen.

In the Country of Poetry

The best teacher I know is a small man named Francis. He is a brilliant and amused man much given to poetry, which issues from him in thick sudden snatches. A talk about rabbits brings forth a rich burst of Blake; politics produces Auden, dry and angry; a casual remark about glowering weather draws forth the marching orotundity of Wordsworth. Sometimes, late in the afternoon, Francis will quietly quote from his own poems, which fill several books. His tongue handles his own lines with the stern affection of a father.

For nearly fifty years Francis has taught literature to college freshmen, whom he calls unscrambled eggs. I suspect his attachment to freshmen is due in part to the fact that they have no idea who he is. He is a shy man. They do not know, on that first day of class, when they find their seats and open their crisp new notebooks and see a small man beaming before them, that he is a priest, that his friend Tom was better known as T. S. Eliot, that his friend Seamus is the poet laureate of Ireland, that he has written things that make people sob, that his heart gave out when he was young and was rebuilt on an operating table, and that he woke up expecting to be dead.

I've never seen him teach; he forbids visitors to his classroom because he believes that both teaching and learning are private acts. But once, I am ashamed to say, I could not refrain from walking by the door of his classroom and snatching a glance at his class in progress. It was spring and the door was flung open. I could hear Francis clearly – he was chanting some lines from Blake, which hung in the air like herons – but all I could see, in that passing instant, was the rapt face of an enormous boy who had taken refuge in the very last row of the old classroom. Though seated where dawdlers and dreamers sit, he neither dawdled nor dreamed; he was engrossed, and he leaned forward on his elbows, straining to catch the velvet mumble of the old poet before him.

Teaching is exuberance and wit, humor and rigor, a sacrifice and a gift. It is the face of a boy in the country of poetry, and the rich song of his teacher spilling his heart in the air.

Last Supper

Emmet's last supper with us was lamb stew, simmered all afternoon with white beans and garlic and tomatoes and oranges, served with spinach salad and fresh-baked bread, accompanied by a red wine from Tuscany. He sang, he told stories. He kept his jacket on during dinner because he was cold, although it was a warm spring evening just after Easter. He removed his fisherman's cap during the meal but put it on again when the dishes were cleared; he was cold, cold. He sang in Gaelic, he sang in English. He sang a song about a mother's love for her children and he sang a song about a whiskey jug. He said grace to open the meal, and blessed my daughter after the meal, placing on her head the same huge hand that had baptized my sons two years before at the very same table, the boys cupped in that gentle slab like fish in a sweet net.

He was very sick then, chilled with the cancer that would soon kill him, with the knowledge of it eating him as he ate the lamb, and he was weak – he had toppled slowly into the ocean of ivy around my house when we arrived, and lay there for a moment like a fallen fir, smiling – but he savored his supper like a starving man, and sipped a little wine in honor of his friend Christ, as he said, and his wit was quick and his memory rich, and when he stood by the door to go, his hand engulfing the knob, he sang a last song, in Gaelic, about calling in the animals at dusk. "I came in with a song and I'll go with a song," he said, and he did.

His last Mass, at Saint Michael's Church in Portland, was packed – people standing in the aisles, children perched on the shoulders of fathers. By then Emmet could barely walk, and he had to choose between standing long enough to say Mass or standing to serve the Eucharist. He chose the Mass, summoning all the gas in his tank to hold the Body of Christ aloft one last time, the thin wafer weighing a thousand pounds. After eating the Lamb himself he sat down in his chair, and while Communion was served by others, he beamed at the hundreds of people who had come to his last supper.

He died five weeks later, on a bright afternoon, called in by the Shepherd he loved so, the God he had served so long and so well with those sinewy hands and silver voice, the God he swore was Irish, for Who better to understand the people of the suffering road? And three days later he was buried in the coffin he had commissioned, of Oregon juniper from the high desert country, and so was laid to rest Michael Emmet Harrington, priest and storyteller, son of a son of County Cork, Emmet who was named for the rebel Robert Emmet, Emmet whose name meant *truth* in Hebrew.

I loved that man, admired the bone of his character and the expansive muscle of his heart, and I sing the long strength of his love, now flung abroad to all the waters and woods of the world. I say to you this morning, Emmet my friend, the Gaelic words you said to all of us so many times, pausing at a door, the knob a knot in the net of your hand: *Go mbeannai Dia thu,* God bless you, God keep you forever.

Notes from a Wake

The priest died on a Monday and was waked Friday night, at his older brother's house. His funeral had been that morning, in the old cathedral, the archbishop presiding, and he'd been buried that afternoon in the city's main Catholic cemetery, Mount Calvary. The funeral procession wound up Mount Calvary along a road built by his father. His father had come from Cork as a teenager. All four of his sons had worked with him at one time or another, carving highways from the woods, laying roads through the city.

On a side table as you entered the older brother's house was the deceased's hammered-silver chalice, black fisherman's cap, tan walking cap, a loaf of fresh soda bread, a pound of roasted coffee beans in a redolent bag, his favorite soft long-sleeved cotton dress shirt, and a posed photograph of his parents, Big John and Blackjack Katie. John and Katie grew up six miles apart in Cork but met in America when Katie spotted John walking to work in the copper mines and said to a friend, "I'll marry that man," and did.

The dining-room table groaned with food, which the deceased had paid for, leaving money in his will for that purpose: a last supper. Beer and wine were out in the backyard, and there was good whiskey in the study.

An old friend rose to speak of the deceased. He is a priest in Montana. His father and the deceased's father were boys together on the coast of Cork. The friend told how their fathers had graduated from school at age twelve: They were coming home over the mountains from the market where they'd sold the families' morning catch, and they decided that it was high time for them to be graduated from school, and so they graduated, right there in the road.

Three of the deceased's young nieces did a step dance on the stones in front of the fireplace.

The priest friend unfolded himself from his chair again and said a poem and then told a story of a fire in Butte in which a Kerryman with wooden legs was caught: "His house was saved but Dinny burned to the ground."

In a corner of the kitchen was an infant at the breast.

The deceased's older brother stood to thank the assemblage for coming to honor the life and memory of his brother, whom he had loved since they were new boys together. The deceased had been best man at his wedding, before the deceased was ordained, and that was the first and last time anyone had ever seen the deceased in a tuxedo.

On the side porch under a cedar tree, a dozen men and two women smoked cigars.

A friend stood to read a short speech about the deceased that noted his enormous hands, quick wit, fluency in Gaelic, long patience, and silver tenor, which he used entering and leaving any domicile: "I came in with a song and I'll leave with a song," he would say, and he did.

The local parish priest, a young man, spoke a long prayer and then led the crowd in a song – "Saint Brendan's Fair Isle," a rouser.

Go mbeannai Dia thu, God bless you, someone said.

Thu? Is there Wicklow in you, then? said a second voice.

Go mbeannai Dia's Muire thu, God and Mary bless you, came the first voice.

Go mbeannai Dia's Muire an Padraig thu, God and Mary and Patrick bless you, said the second voice, and then both voices laughed.

The deceased's younger brother did a slow jig on the stones in front of the fireplace.

Three of the deceased's many nephews stood by the fireplace and eerily and accurately brought back the voices and gestures of the deceased and then Big John and Blackjack Katie, the deceased's deceased parents, whom very nearly everyone in the room had known.

The Montana priest stood again and told a story about an Anglican bishop touring through Cork. The bishop stops to chat with an old farmer, a Catholic. "Do ye have many Protestants here?" asks the bishop. "Not so many," says the farmer. "It's the rabbits are the *real* pests."

The family counted how many of them had been baptized by the deceased: forty-seven. Number of family marriages celebrated by the deceased: fourteen. Number of family funerals, three: his mother, his father, and his youngest brother, dead too young.

A nephew rose to recount the deceased's professional career: teacher and dean at the local Catholic high school, principal of a second Catholic high school, director of education for the archdiocese, organizer for a Catholic education association, pastor at two large parishes. The deceased retired but three years ago, and wished to spend his time on his bicycle and in the Holy Land and Ireland and Mexico, and reading and photographing, and walking through the woods where he had fished and trapped as a boy wild along the rivers during the summers his father cut a sinuous road through a deep fir forest as silent and huge as a green cathedral, and eating long dinners with friends, and finishing a scholarly project about the Mass rocks of Ireland, where hedge priests celebrated furtive Masses under the sharp eyes of the British soldiers enforcing the Penal Laws, and where the hedge priests were not so occasionally shot dead by soldiers; there was one such Mass rock in Ireland where the priest had been shot dead before he finished the Mass, and the deceased very much wished to journey again to Ireland and at that rock finish that Mass, so long paused – but he died.

The family counted how many of them were around the deceased when he died, five days ago: twenty.

By now it was past midnight. Children were draped on shoulders like scarves. People went home in bunches. The beer and wine came in from the backyard and the kitchen was cleaned. The food on the dining-room table was packed up and put away and given away on sopping paper plates. The deceased's possessions stayed where they were on the side table. The deceased's younger brother and sister embraced the older brother and went home. The older brother's wife, who had loved the deceased, went up to bed, and then a minute later so did the older brother, and that was the end of Emmet's wake.

A Thin Ragged Man

Several months ago a man named Walter appeared at our door. He was a slight ragged man, gaunt, dirty, polite. He worked hard all day in the basement, sheetrocking walls and building a wooden floor. He worked hard all the next day too. The third day he barely worked at all. He spent the day eating sandwiches and talking about himself. He had served three tours in Vietnam, some of them in a psychiatric ward. He said that he had a wife and child but they left him, that someone had recently stolen his truck and tools, that he was grateful for the work in our basement.

On the first day he had estimated the cost of his work and we agreed on a price. I bought all the supplies and borrowed tools. On the second day he asked for an advance and got it. On the third day he asked for another advance and got it. He also asked for a raincoat and a ride into the city and got them too. I dropped him off in the city; my daughter and I waved to him as he shuffled off.

That was the last we saw of Walter for a while. I returned the tools. Two weeks later he showed up and worked hard all day again. He said he'd badly underbid the job and asked for another advance. We said no. His face fell. He was out on the streets, he said, and needed to find ten dollars a day for his methadone shot. We said no. He saw my wife's beloved old backpack and sleeping bag and proposed that he finish the job in exchange for them. Okay, said my wife. At the end of the day Walter walked off into a howling thunderstorm carrying the pack and bag and we never saw him again.

Walter is a thief, a hapless ragged polite thief, a liar, a heroin addict. I hate him. He stole our money, left the basement a shambles, reduced my wife to tears at the waste of money and time. I hate that he held my children, that he shook hands with my wife, that he ever set foot in my home. But if I believe that the gaunt ragged man who died between thieves on the Hill of Skulls was reborn, I have to look for Him in Walter. This is very difficult for me. But as long as love wriggles out of hate, there is faith.

The preceding essay was first published in Portland, *the quarterly magazine of the University of Portland, in its Spring 1996 issue. A few weeks later I received a letter from Jim Wood, a prisoner at the Eastern Oregon Correctional Institution, who has given permission for his letter to appear with my essay.*

Dear Mr. Doyle,

As a rule I avoid writing people I do not know; but, after reading "A Thin Ragged Man" in *Portland* for Spring of '96, I feel compelled to write you. Please bear with me as I struggle with my emotions and the difficulty of expressing them, along with my thoughts, to a person who is a stranger to myself and my experiences.

Why do I feel so compelled to write you? Because I believe that you want to follow God's instruction and Christ's example to love and forgive, from that love, those who trespass against you. I believe that I know enough about Walter, for I am a man much like him, to help you.

When I read "A Thin Ragged Man," I felt an immediate pull, a connection with all of you. You see, Mr. Doyle, I too am an addict like Walter. I have struggled even in the deepest, most desperate times to throw off the chains of addiction, only to fail. I, like Walter, have tried to salvage sanity and my humanity through honest labor and reaching out for some connection to "normal" people, only to fail because of my own feelings of inadequacy, shame, and apartness. Please believe, Mr. Doyle, I am not writing you to complain about my life. I believe that you truly meant what you said, "as long as love wriggles out of hate, there is faith." I believe you hate Walter right now. I believe that you don't want to do so. I also believe that love grows from knowledge, understanding and (mostly) empathy. So, please, let me tell you about Walter.

Walter, too, hates the life he lives. He knows what he has become – "a hapless, ragged, polite thief, a liar, a heroin addict" – and every day he curses the self-made choices that brought him to that point in life; and, because those choices were self-made, he hates himself. Can you imagine the shame he felt sitting in your house? This man wanted to work honestly to support himself, maybe even to begin the slow march back. Knowing all that Walter has lost over the years – spiritual strength, family, home, self-respect, dignity, ad infinitum – it is not hard for me to feel the terrible ache, emptiness and shame that he felt.

You see, Mr. Doyle, every moment that he was in your home, Walter compared himself to you. He saw not what you have, but what he has lost, and it tore him apart. Walter had probably just gotten "clean"; otherwise, he could not have worked diligently for a half-day, let alone two full

days, in your basement. Without the warm, numbing emo-
tion-dampening blanket of heroin and much experience
in dealing with real emotions, can you imagine the turmoil
Walter was in? He may not have had adequate experience
in dealing with them, but he sure knew how to kill the pain
and the shame; hence the "advances."

The lie Walter told himself was that he could leave that
second day, numb his pain with "just one" and be all right.
Imagine the added shame as it sunk in the next day as he
sat in your home relating to you all, while he tried to work
up the courage to ask for another advance, just how impossible is was to do "just one." Imagine also that Walter knows
that he has disappointed and hurt you; he does, and it is one
more ache that he will use to beat himself emotionally
about the head and shoulders. Do not believe that Walter
came to your family's home to con you or to steal from
you. The fact that he is hated for his actions is evidence
that he took from you emotionally as well as financially.

This letter is *not* for Walter's benefit. He and his life will
improve only through much clean time, appropriate treat-
ment, and God's grace. I pray that he either gets into detox
or gets arrested to begin the journey. This letter is for you
and your family. If you must hate, hate the behavior, not
the man. Understand that as poor, ragged, and hapless a
thief as Walter is, he is a man who truly wants not to be as
he is. Pray that your wife's "beloved old backpack and
sleeping bag" are keeping him warm and carrying his few
possessions safely. Someday he may forgive himself and he
will seek to make amends. Love the man and Christ will
shine forth through you.

For now, please allow me to apologize to you for Walter. I know that he wants to himself. Mr. Doyle, God bless you and your family.

Sincerely,
Jim Wood

Christ's Elbows

Or, A Note on the Sheer Cathartic Physical Exuberance of Christ, with Especial Attention Paid to His Wiry Son-of-a-Carpenter's Pointed Angry Elbows

Lost, usually, in the awe and mystery of stories of Christ the Lord of the Starfields is the sheer coltish *physicalness* of Christ the wiry young man, at the peak of his professional and physical career in his early thirties, before the events that ended his life suddenly at age thirty-three.

Accounts of his body in action are few and far between. Luke gives us an early glimpse of the boy Jesus, who "grew and became strong," and "grew in stature," and we may imagine him hauling lumber for his stepfather, and straining to curve planks for chairs, and the assorted other labors of a carpenter's apprentice, not to mention the various physical tasks around the house to which he was set by his mother, who loved him like crazy but still needed some strong-backed young help digging in the garden, sweeping the kitchen floor, washing clothes, etc.

And we may further imagine him in the unaccounted time between his twelfth year, when he scared his parents half to death by staying behind in Jerusalem and gabbing with the rabbis in the Temple, and his thirtieth, when he entered public life by plunging into the Jordan River and watching his brusque cousin John's hairy arm douse him with baptismal water. Perhaps he ran through the fields for miles at dusk to shake off his restless teenage energy, perhaps he relished competitive fisticuffs with his jumpy, energetic friends, perhaps he sprang over high stone walls with the coiled muscularity of a basketball player. For all we know he was a terrific athlete, not at all the polite quiet simpering mama's boy that centuries of devotional painters would have us admire.

But for the most part we have to invent his athleticism, because there is a notable paucity of physical references to Christ in the Scriptures. This is easily understood; the various authors of the Gospels wished to recount tales of the Christ that would reveal both his unique divinity and his many (fascinatingly phrased) suggestions for right living and eternal salvation. And because the Gospels are not eyewitness accounts, but quasi-historical essays very much meant to persuade and convert, they lack an eyewitness's attention to their subject's physical presence: carriage, bearing, bounciness of stride, height, weight, injuries, the strength of his handshake, the length of his fingers (did his hand swallow the hand of the Garasene girl he raised from the dead? Could he palm the heads of the children who followed him like puppies?), the weight of his hand on the shoulders and faces of the men and women he healed with his touch.

So mostly what we see of the physical Christ in the Gospels, until his last herculean hauling of the cross, is the travelin' man – walking, walking, walking, all over Judea, sitting down to teach, getting up to move off when he is done, reclining here and there before a meal, but then up again and out the door and back to the road, go go go, the man was relentless, the preacher with no off button. We might well picture Christ with the thin hard body of a marathon racer, all bones and ropy muscles, considering the miles he racked up in three years; we might also better understand why the washing of feet was such a momentous ritual at the time, especially for Christ, who must have sighed many a night when he stared down at the worn and dusty pins that had carried him so far so fast.

But there is one hour in his life when we see a flash of utter furious physical action on Christ's part, an hour when this most curious of men must have experienced the sheer joyous exuberance of a young mammal in full flight: when he lets himself go and flings over the first money changer's table in the Temple at Jerusalem, coins flying, doves thrashing into the air, oxen bellowing, sheep yowling, the money changer going head-over-teakettle, all heads turning, *what the . . . ?* You don't think Christ got a shot of utter child-like physical *glee* at that moment? Too late to stop now, his rage rushing to his head, his veiny carpenter's-son wiry arms and hard feet milling as he whizzes through the Temple overturning tables, smashing birdcages, probably popping a furious money changer here and there with a quick left jab or a well-placed Divine Right Elbow to the money-lending teeth, whipping his scourge of cords against the billboard-size flank of an ox, men scrambling to get out of the way, to grab some of the flying coins, to get a punch in on this nutty rube causing all the ruckus. . . .

In all this holy rage and chaos, don't you think there was a little absolute boyish mindless physical jittery joy in the guy?

Think of the *man* for a second, not the eternal Son of Light; remember that this most riveting of figures was equally God and man; and then put yourself in his place, halfway through the roiling roaring riot of the Temple that day. Things are completely out of hand, utter disorder, and he knows in his heart that there will be hell to pay, so to speak, when he's done tearing the place apart. But he also knows he's right, and that he is fulfilling the prophecy laid out for him ("zeal for Thy house will consume me") and for once in his careful, marching-toward-eternity-and-salvation-of-all life he's let Himself go utterly, he's *not* being careful, he's on a rocking, socking, cathartic roll, he's unstoppable, his elbows are flying like a professional basketball player's; and I bet a buck he was grinning from ear to Christly ear.

And God bless him for it.

The moment would end, of course, and the cops would come, figuratively speaking, and he would have a tense exchange with the men he'd just thrown out of the Temple (moderates on each side holding back the combatants as they strained to get in one more blow, the veins in their necks bulging as they yell at each other), and he would resume the life and work that rivet us to this day. But I smile whenever I think of him wading into the seething mass of prim bankers in the Temple, and upending their world with a broad grin on his face. So he upends our world, over and over, every single day if we are lucky and attentive, and it is a grace upon us if we smile as our own prim plans for making money and careful living go flying all to pieces.

Perhaps the chaos of our plans is the shadow of his smile.

Have You Anything Here to Eat?

Reading the New Testament does not have to be a religious experience, nor does the interested reader have to be religiously motivated. It is a fascinating collection of essays, filled with riveting tales of human nature – including the human nature of this curious Christ fellow.

Luke, for example, tells of Christ getting to the table twice in His last earthly moments: once in the company of Cleopas and his friend, with whom Christ had walked the road from Jerusalem to Emmaus, and then again in the company of (in a poignant phrase that makes us think of Judas's horrible loneliness) "the eleven" remaining Apostles. With Cleopas and his companion, Christ takes bread, blesses it, breaks it, and hands it to His friends, at which point their brains snap awake and they recognize their Savior – but He "vanishes from their sight" without getting any bread.

They rush back to Jerusalem to tell the Apostles, and while they are stumbling over themselves to get their story out, Christ suddenly appears again. This gives everyone the willies, and a patient Christ lets them touch his hands and feet, to prove that he is real, and then Christ gets to the important matter at hand:

"Have you anything here to eat?" He asks, politely.

Indeed they do, broiled fish in fact, and Christ finally gets a meal.

John's version of Christ's real last supper is a little different. He tells the story of Christ appearing on the shore of the Sea of Tiberias. Peter and several companions have spent the night fishing, to no avail. At dawn they are hailed by a fellow on the shore, who tells them to cast in one particular spot. They do, hauling in exactly 153 fish. ("Large fish," too, notes John.) When they land their catch, they notice that the fellow has laid a fire and started fish and bread cooking.

"Come and have breakfast," says Christ, equably.

Clearly there are textual and theological reasons for Christ's desire for something to eat. The authors of the Gospels wanted to show that Christ was *physically* alive after his murder, fully alive in His body, not a spirit or a dream, and they wanted to show Him again breaking bread in sacramental fashion, so as to cement this ritual as the means by which Christ appears in the Eucharist.

But there is a wonderful simple human reality to Christ's hunger. The man is *famished*. He's missed meals for three days, He has a lot on His mind, He's on His way back to heaven, but before He goes He is itching for a nice piece of broiled fish and a little bread on the side with the men and women He loves. Do we not like Him the more for his prandial persistence? And think for a moment about the holiness of our own food, and the ways that cooking and sharing a meal can be forms of love and prayer. And realize again that the Eucharist at the heart of stubborn Catholicism is the breakfast that Christ prepares for Catholics, every morning, as we return from fishing in vast dreamy seas?

three³

Glory Bee

I had the rare pleasure recently of a private Mass; that is, a Mass at which there were only two people, not counting Christ, who arrived during the Eucharist. There was the priest, and there was me.

Outside the room there were two sparrows also, and inside the room, it turned out later, was a bee. I believe it was the common honey bee, *Apis mellifera,* and not one of its cousins, *Api dorsata, floreata, cerana,* or *laboriosa,* but I didn't get close enough for an especially good look and neither did the priest.

The Mass was in a room in a residence hall at a college because I had not been able to find a Mass being said elsewhere during a day in which we, the priest and I, had been thrown together in the social ramble, and as each of us did not wish to go a Sunday without spiritual sustenance and the nutritious central ritual of our faith, I found a room in a residence hall, and the priest found the materials necessary, as he said, for him to say Mass, and so he did.

The bee lifted off from a windowsill just as the priest finished preparing his cruets of water and wine and opened his book to begin Mass. It began to fly due north, toward the table where Mass was about to commence, and it did not fly in a straight line, but in a series of short zigzags, not unlike repetitive dance steps. It is interesting to note in this

53

regard that *Apis mellifera,* like all honey bees, conducts a dance to inform its mates of food sources. There are three dances: the round dance, the sickle dance (used only by the Italian race of *mellifera*), and the waggle dance. The dances may indicate meals as far away as one thousand meters.

The meal of the Mass began. Opening prayers, first reading, second reading, the bee is still aloft, Gospel reading, the bee subsides, the creed, intercessions, the bringing forth of the gifts by yours truly, the bee is up, Communion, the bee is down, concluding blessing, the bee is up, the Mass is ended, the bee is down, go in peace, the bee is cutting dance steps in the air.

The words in the air with the bee have been powerful and spare, as simple and sweet and dangerous as the bee, as potentially painful and penetrating, like nails through palms. The priest has sung and chewed the words as if they were poems, which they are, and I heard them as if for the first time, my mind circling and waggling, remembering the days many years ago when I was a child standing in a church with the Mass washing over me like a sea of sound, a child picking up a fallen word here and there, and from these spent beautiful bees falling around me, *Apis mellifera* in the autumns of their days, the words falling on the pews on the floor on the shoulders of the men and women around me, I built a story about the Mass, about sweet-stinging Christ, about the God I heard and smelled but could never see, about believing against all reason and rationality that once God showed His sad radiant brown bearded Judean face and danced upon this earth and put Aramaic words into the dusty air, and then I heard other stories and stitched them into our story too, and then after many years I am standing in a room after a private Mass and thinking that the Mass, stripped to its bones, is a fiercely persistent memoir, a naked meal for a naked carpenter, an act of exuberant joy that He lived and died and lived. How apt that this Mass be said over a circling bee and two birds as well as one stung man: for the Mass brings all creatures together in and under the Word, which was in the beginning, which has no end, which will always bee.

A Sunday, in October,
Under a Flight of Geese

A little Catholic university chapel, all cedar and sunlight, amid a riot of rhododendrons.

Behind the chapel a crowd of muscular old oak trees.

Before it a sea of fresh-cut grass dotted with scrawny cherry trees, toddlers, dandelions.

Above it a ragged arrowhead of geese, southing.

Sounds: pants legs scissoring toward Mass, small talk by the front door, chirping children, a metronomic phoebe, Bach's organ fugue in C minor.

Inside: a small child with his right arm in the baptismal font up to his shoulder. Child's father turns and notices his son's oar in the water; father emits indescribable sound, carts boy off to dry pew.

Mass begins, gently.

There are perhaps 150 people here this morning, the great majority of them undergraduates, although it's an all-ages show, and from the balcony where I ride herd on my three small children I see gray hair, white hair, green hair, blue hair, no hair.

My children, interested and hungry, eat crackers.

"This morning we gather as a faith community to broaden our vision," says the young priest. He will utter the word *community* seven times this morning, by my count, and tribal binding is the clear theme of this Mass. Two other priests are robed and on the altar, and the whole crowd sings lustily, holds hands while chanting the Our Father, exchanges Hearty Handshakes of Peace at startling length (one energetic boy making his way completely around the chapel). All but a handful will receive Communion; all but a handful will stay after Mass to chat in cheerful knots; all, apparently, are excited and stimulated by Mass. This crowd isn't dutiful; it's pumped. Rumors of death of faith among youth greatly exaggerated, at least this morning.

The Gospel, from Mark, is about the Apostles James and John, who itch for good seats in heaven and demand same of the Rabbi. Christ fires back classic Christly conundrum: he who wishes to be great must be a servant.

Homily: "Not the most flattering portrait of James and John, is it? They ask for prestige and power, and Christ rebukes them sharply, as he rebukes us, all these years later, as we itch for power, too. Be honest: Don't you wish for status among your peers? Don't you want to be first and best? We're more like James and John than we like to admit, and as usual Christ disturbs us. . . ."

My children, having marched through crackers and ginger snaps, are now eating grapes.

Eucharist: At the moment of transformation the priest pauses for a tremulous instant, and the whole chapel is riveted and silent as he hoists *I am who am* aloft; and then comes the Communion shuffle, the sharp smell of mediocre wine, dry crackers on tongues, another hymn, and the ranks of bowed meditating heads, blessing and dismissal, *another* hymn, and then the organ groans awake and sends us out again into the light, where the phoebe is still keeping time, and for no reason, every reason, I am delighted, my pockets filled with grapes, my pinkies gripped by small boys, my morning mad with miracles.

Father, Son, Spirit Holy

Dinner hour, and I sit down to table with my wife and three small children, ready to talk turkey. Today it is my youngest son's turn for grace, and he starts us off with the Sign of the Cross. He has a unique take on this act, as in so many other aspects of his life: Not unlike a third-base coach, he makes a flurry of motions, touching forehead, belly, shoulders, nose, temples, ears, and (finally) tongue, all the while chanting, at a terrific pace, *Father, Son, Spirit Holy.*

As usual, he sends his family into stitches, and after a while we bring him around to a slightly more orthodox Sign of the Cross, but as his mother and sister and brother recover from the giggles and set to work editing their meals, his father's mind, as usual, rambles. Whence came this unusual motion of the hand, and incantation? Why do we mark moments great and small, holy and horrendous, with this gentle handmade echo of the crucifix? *Father, Son, Holy Ghost,* I whispered as a boy, and *Father, Son, Holy Spirit,* I whisper as a man, in moments of joy and fear, prayer and penitence, before a meal, during the Mass, after a death. I make the Sign of the Cross in wonder, when my children do or say something that slaps me into remembering they came to me from the hand of the Lord. I make the sign in gratitude when they finally fall asleep. I make it in desperate prayer when they are wan and weak and sick.

I make it before meals, during Masses, after funerals, after baptisms, I make it in awe and epiphany and tragedy.

I do it all the time, and I am by no means alone; no other simple physical gesture is so widespread among Catholics. More than sinking to our knees, more than folding our hands together in prayer, more than bowing our heads under blessings, it is the making of the Sign of the Cross with our hands that marks us as Catholics – as men and women (and small children) who believe in the Risen Christ, the god and man who died on a wooden crucifix on the Hill of Skulls, long centuries ago.

Scholars trace the practice as far back as the year 110, by which time it was already established as a common gesture among Christians – most common, apparently, among those Christian communities associated with Saint Paul. "Its format is a simple geometry," says the Congregation of Holy Cross theologian Father Jeffrey Sobosan. "It traces out a cross in the sequence of four points touched: head to chest, shoulder to shoulder. The early Christians thought it was the way Jesus *died,* far more than the way He *lived* prior to His arrest, that constituted the saving act whereby He pleased God." So those early Christian cults honored, in a simple physical gesture, the geometric shape on which Christ gave His life for us. It is a small miracle, perhaps, that this gesture has persisted unchanged throughout many nations and centuries; but then again, miracles are not unusual, are they?

Such a simple act, our hands cutting the air like the wings of birds, fingers alighting gently on our bodies in memory of the body broken for us:

Father, we say, touching our heads, the seats of our cerebrations, and we think of the Maker, that vast incomprehensible coherence stitching everything together, and

Son, touching our hearts, and feeling the ache and exhaustion of the Father's Son, the God-made-man, the gaunt dusty tireless fellow who walked and talked endlessly through the hills of Judea, who knew what would happen to Him, who accepted it with amazing grace, who died screaming that we might live past death, and

Holy, touching the left shoulder, on which we carry hope, and

Spirit, touching the right shoulder, on which we carry love, and the gesture is done, hanging in the air like a memory, its line traced on my body as if printed there by the thousands of times my hand has marked it. I make it in the dark, over my sleeping children; I make it at dawn, staring at the incredible world waking; I make it smiling, cheered by the persistence of miracles; I make it sobbing over the corpse of a friend in a wooden coffin, returned now to the Carpenter who made him.

Simple, powerful, poignant, the Sign of the Cross is a mnemonic device like the Mass, in which we sit down to table with one another and remember the Last Supper, or a baptism, where we remember John the Baptist's brawny arm pouring some of the Jordan River over Christ. So we remember the central miracle and paradox of the faith that binds us each to each: that we believe, against all evidence and sense, in life and love and light, in the victory of those things over death and evil and darkness.

Such a ferocious and brave notion, to be hinted at by such a simple motion, and the gesture itself lasting perhaps all of four seconds, if you touch all the bases and don't rush. But simple as the Sign of the Cross is, it carries a brave weight: It names the Trinity, celebrates the Creator, and brings home all the power of faith to the brush of fingers on skin and bone and belly. So do we, sometimes well and sometimes ill, labor to bring home our belief in God's love to the stuff of our daily lives, the skin and bone of this world — and the Sign of the Cross helps us to remember that we have a Companion on the road.

A Note on Epiphanies

Between January 5 (feast day of the legendarily energetic John Neumann, bishop of Philadelphia) and January 7 (feast day of Raymond of Penyafort, who lived to be one hundred years old and was sentenced for a time to auditing the financial transactions of the Vatican, which task alone probably was enough for sainthood), there is the feast of the Epiphany, one of the oldest and most mysterious in the Church. These days we treat it mostly as the end of the twelve days of Christmas, and on Epiphany we strike the Christmas tree and vacuum the needles it has shed and push the ottoman back where it was, but we miss a rare chance to stare our faith in the face if we treat Epiphany as merely the day that we haul the noble fir to the curb.

Epiphany is also called the feast of the Three Wise Men, and the Gospel of the day relates the familiar tale of Gaspar, Melchior, and Balthasar, who came to Jerusalem from "the East" – perhaps Arabia, Chaldea, or Persia – seeking the infant King of the Jews: "We saw His star at its rising and have come to pay Him homage." Their close attention to rising stars is the reason many scholars think that these three weary travelers may well have been astrologers, stunned by the advent of a new star, and driven by angels or curiosity or fear to march many miles in search of the King of Stars, whom they find mewling in straw and attended by the gentle beasts of the barnyard.

For them this Child was an epiphany, a revelation, a tear in the fabric of the world they knew, and so He is for us, too, all these centuries later. Epiphany, like Easter, cuts right to the heart of the unbelievable story we believe: There was a child born in a cold, dusty shed, and this child was made of the stuff that made the stars; and this child became a man who walked many miles to teach us that love would save our souls; and to salve our sins he died between two thieves at Golgotha, and three days later was brought to life, because he was God and man.

Ludicrous.

But true; and His coming was an epiphany then, a revelation of the inscrutable Mind that governs all things. And it is an epiphany now, on Epiphany, and all through the year, and all through the years, from our own days mewling in our mothers' arms through the many miles we travel wearily looking for rising stars.

A Note on Kneeling

It wasn't until I could no longer kneel that I began to savor the lovely simplicity of the ancient act, and guess at its provenance, and savor its humility, and notice it not only in Mass but in many other aspects of life – proposing marriage, laboring in the garden, accepting knighthood, burying the bird slain by the cat, retrieving socks that have leaped from the overburdened laundry basket, listening to very small children.

So simple an act, the folding of the body unto its knees, and done in as many idiosyncratic ways as there are idiosyncratic human beings. At Mass these days, no longer quite supple enough to fold that far, I sit back in my pew as the rest of the congregation begins to kneel (the lovely staccato sound of crashing kneelers echoing throughout the church) and wince as my children flop to their knees with the careless recklessness of the rubbery young, and watch entranced as my wife contracts with her usual pliant grace, and empathize with the old and sore as they slowly creak to their knees like old horses closing up shop for the night.

Kneeling must have originated first as a gesture of submission to greater power; the Catholic theologian Jeffrey Sobosan has observed that kneeling really is a presentation of the head, the seat of all five senses, to a higher authority – an offering of your head as acknowledgement of that person's or Person's sway over your very life. Think of the decapitation ritual, for example, which requires kneeling by the condemned so that the executioner can get a good angle on the head of the unfortunate executionee. (Saint Thomas More was famous for his courtesy in presenting his head to his decapitator, as was the great Roman orator and statesman Cicero.)

Curtsying, bowing from the waist, genuflecting, and bowing the head alone are all diminished variations of kneeling – minor-league kneelings, as it were, mini-kneelings, gestures toward kneeling – but all as a family are acts of reverence, awe, gratitude, supplication, and submission before the presence or idea or sign of the Creator. So the body bends before the blessed, and we act out the reverence we feel before the King of Kings and His works and creations – in the Mass, in confession, at novenas, in moments of prayer, sometimes while looking for socks.

Mostly the act is deliberate, but sometimes it is a reaction: I have seen people forced to their knees by news of sudden death, by the birth of a child, even once by the stunning presence – or, more accurately, the stunning absence – of the Grand Canyon, seen for the first time in a long life.

We are not the only creatures to bend before our betters: Many biologists have noted that submission to a dominant being is a trait of many mammals, particularly the more intelligent and social ones, and the great American biologist Edward O. Wilson has speculated (in his book *Consilience*) that the elaborate signals of respect used in religion are close cousins to the hierarchical semiotics of higher mammals as well as hallmarks of religious groups' evolutionary success as close-knit communities.

I am struck not by the biological semiotics of kneeling, however, but by the sheer poetry and clarity of the act. Faced with the awesome, we drop to our knees, we deliberately reduce ourselves, we abandon at least some of our precious status and power. On a high hill in Massachusetts once, by the sea, I fell to my knees to propose marriage, for what I felt would be the only time in my life, a moment of enormous power and mystery. And because a remarkable woman said *yes* on that hill, on a beautiful May day, I have knelt often since, mostly to console our children, or to see what they saw, or to arrive at their level so that we might converse and regard each other as equals, rather than as child and remote awesome Father. A friend of mine knelt once to listen carefully to my small daughter, a quiet act I have always remembered as a courtesy to her, a sign of his egolessness and his respect.

In a way, Jesus Christ is Himself a sort of respectful kneeling on the part of God the Father, is He not? The Father inclined to our level by sending His Son as one of us, God made man by woman, a thin dusty prickly confusing Jewish preacher before whom people kneel left and right in the Gospels — as we kneel before Him today (in Mass, during the sacraments, at ritual and casual moments of awe and power); and as we kneel before saints, as men and women privileged to have lived and died His message so completely; as we kneel, occasionally, still, before popes and cardinals and bishops and priests and nuns and brothers and monks and deacons, in respect for the way they have given their lives and talents to trouble others for

Christ; and as we kneel, occasionally, before one another, as miracles who house the love of Christ in our hearts, not to mention our bony lovely knees.

Massing

Christmas is nearly upon us, and with it will come a sudden swelling in the Catholic population at Mass. To the familiar pews come unfamiliar faces, and what was a generally reedy chorus of responses during Mass is suddenly robust with too-hearty voices a touch behind the pace. Occasional Catholics are back in church during the Christmas season; easily recognized by the way they slowly re-accustom themselves to the words and actions of the Mass, they are drawn irresistibly back to the Church and church of their parents and pasts, to the church they may have seen only during Christmas Mass or their wedding ceremony or when their children were baptized there. We may stare at them wonderingly, and ask silently why they come just this once, why they choose to miss the chance at daily miracle that is the Mass, why they descend, well-dressed and sitting in the front, at the stunning ceremony they miss the other 364 days of the year; but we have missed many a Mass, too, and so stare first at ourselves.

We welcome them because they are here to partake of Him with us, they are our brothers and sisters and neighbors, they are us. Perhaps we wish they would enjoy the simple poetry of a quiet daily Mass here and there, and not take that second pew that affords us such a lovely view of the whole panoply of miracles in the Mass, the Eucharist on high and the sleepy altar girl below, the brazen gleam of altarware and the simplicity of a cotton alb, but all in all a full church is a good thing, and if we are pushed to the back or forced to stand by a tide of our fellows, then we will be silent, and offer it up to God, as our mothers used to ask us to do, because we love our mothers, and His Mother, and Him, too, which is why we are all at Mass, regulars and irregulars alike.

The gaunt ragged man who died and was reborn gave us the Mass so that we would remember Him, and eat His body again and again, and so be saved. That the Mass binds us each to each as brothers and sisters in His name is also the point. So when we walk happily into the church on Christmas morning, and discover that our pew is filled, and the bulletins are all taken, and we are jostled rudely from the door by a river of unfamiliar folk, we will smile suddenly, and remember that He died for all of us.

Washed Clean

"The rain is raining all around, it falls on field and tree, it rains on the umbrellas here, and on the ships at sea," wrote Robert Louis Stevenson of the Scottish rain, a century ago. Here in the Pacific Northwest the autumnal rains have begun to spill from the sky, and water sluices over land and people, cleansing both, reminding us that we begin in water, are baptized by water, are composed of water. Water is our cousin and our cousin is back in town for a few months, his burbling visit forcing us back inside house and heart, back to a chair by the fire, back to contemplation of the ways of water in the stories of the Son who came to us.

One turns to Matthew's Gospel for close accounting of Christ and the waters of the Jordan – waters poured on His brow by a curious and prickly soul so sure that water was the means of salvation that his name has descended to us as John the Baptist. Christ asks John to baptize Him with the running waters of a river, that most relentless of scouring creatures.

"I have need to to be baptized by You, and do You come to *me?*" asks John, savage and rude John, John who has just baptized Pharisees and Sadducees while audibly gritting his teeth and lashing them with his razor tongue in a speech that begins with "You brood of vipers!" and then gets less polite, John of the "garment of camel's hair, and a leather belt about his waist, and his food was locusts and wild honey," as Matthew reports, ever the careful journalist.

"Permit it at this time," says Jesus, calmly; "for in this way it is fitting for us to fulfill all righteousness." And so on His brow John pours the waters of the Jordan, the mighty river of Judea.

"And after being baptized," writes Matthew, "Jesus went up immediately from the water; and behold, the heavens were opened, and he saw the Spirit of God descending as a dove, and coming upon Him, and behold there was a voice out of the heavens, saying, 'This is My beloved Son, in whom I am well pleased.'"

Staring out the window at the gray corduroy sky one thinks of that stern Voice, falling down in praise upon His Son, and suddenly the rafts of rain do not seem onerous but holy, do not seem an affliction but an extraordinary gift; this is the water of life, and we drink from it so that we may live, in Him, with Him, until the waters part and there is nothing but Light.

Name-Calling

If ever there was a word that seemed to shout its antecedents, it is *Jesuit,* the name applied to the members of the Society of Jesus. "Jesuit" is patently "man of Jesus," is it not?

Well, no.

Etymologically the word *Jesuit* can be traced through the French *Jesuite* to the Latin *Iesus,* which itself comes from the Hebrew *yeshu'a,* a contraction of *yehoshu'a,* or "help of Jehovah." One may even speculate that the early Christians were occasionally called Iesus-ites, or something of the sort, by the Romans; the urge to apply a general label to groups of people is an ancient and irresistable impulse, and imperial Rome did a good deal of it, partly out of racism and partly because the empire included a lot of peoples and races and nationalities and religions, and labels made commerce and war more easily transactable.

It was in the 1530s that ten "friends in the Lord" coalesced around the charismatic Basque Inigo de Onaz y Loyola. These friends formally chose an organizational name in late 1537, when three of the company went to Rome and the others scattered around northern Italy, to preach, hear confessions, and do a little quiet recruiting among local students.

"This last [objective] brought up the question as to what name they should bear in case they were asked who they were," wrote Martin Harney, SJ, in *The Jesuits in History*. It was Inigo, the former military man, who assumed command of the situation and firmly named the band of brothers: "You will say that you belong to the Company of Jesus, that will be our name," he said, and that was that. Harney notes that some scholars were so impressed by Ignatius's insistence on nomenclature that they concluded the name was revealed to him in a vision. "But the statements of the early Jesuits are conflicting on this point, and so nothing positive can be asserted."

Ignatius used the common military parlance of his day in so naming his spiritual team (small bands of soldiers were commonly called companies, and usually took the name of their leader), and "company" is actually a more accurate translation of Ignatius's organizational idea than "society," the word that had been used for many centuries to describe the Jesuit order. Be that as it may, in 1541, when the company was formally chartered in Rome and Inigo was elected superior general, they were ecclesiastically christened *societas* – a not especially accurate Latin translation of the word *company*, but Society they became and Society they remain.

In the streets of Rome, however, they were known by other names. Some already called them Jesuits, and they were also called the Reformed Priests, or sometimes the Theatines, by people who confused them with the men of another newly founded order. John O'Malley, SJ, in his fine book *The First Jesuits*, notes that they were called Ignatians in Spain – *ignistae* or *ignatiani*. In Paris they were the

Iniguistas (men of Inigo). And as they spread abroad, vig-
orously preaching "in churches, in the open air (with
bonfires on the hills to summon the audience), on the street
corners, in public squares and markets, and hospitals, pris-
ons, playing fields and dockside," as historian John Padberg,
SJ, has written, they acquired names as various as the countries they traveled. Perhaps the most dignified of these titles
was the Apostles, which is what they were called in Portu-
gal and in the East Indies – countries where the Jesuits
were considered kinsmen of Saint Francis Xavier, a hero
to the Portuguese.

Although the word *Jesuit* apparently made its first
formal appearance in the fourteenth century, when the
religious body founded by Blessed Giovanni Colombini
was named the Gesuati, the first documented use of it as
applied to members of the Society was in 1545, when
Peter Canisius noted in a letter that Protestants in Cologne
were using the word to denigrate their Catholic adver-
saries. By the end of the sixteenth century the Jesuits
themselves had taken up the term informally, although
Harney notes that neither the Society nor the popes have
ever used the word in official documents – *clerics of the Society of Jesus* is the preferred papal term in bulls and such.

Interestingly, the phrase *Society of Jesus* stayed contro-
versial for centuries. There were some objections to it even
in 1540, on the grounds that Pope Pius II had already insti-
tuted a short-lived military order under that name in 1458.
In 1561 the Society was recognized in France only under
the name Society of the College of Clermont (the Jesuits'
first Parisian house), because the Parliament of Paris
objected to the use of Jesus' name in a bureaucratic title.

Pope Sixtus V was preparing to change the Jesuits' name to Society of the Jesuits when he died; his sucessor, Pope Gregory XIV, settled the matter in an apostolic constitution called *Ecclesiae Catholicae* (1591), in which he said, flatly, "the name Society of Jesus by which this praiseworthy order was called by the Apostolic See at its birth, and by which it has been designated hitherto, is to be retained for all times."

It is entertaining to ponder that the Society of Jesus could, with a couple of twists of fate, be called the Company of Ignatius. Imagine calling the Jesuits as a whole "the Company" – an ominously cold title that sounds like something from the pages of George Orwell or a John Grisham thriller.

A Note on the Death of the
Index Librorum Prohibitorum

In 1966 the Catholic Church ceased publication of the *Index Librorum Prohibitorum (Index of Prohibited Books),* the list of banned books that began with an Index of Forbidden Works promulgated by Gelasius in Rome in the year 496. The Christian habit of attempting to regulate the reading of the faithful went even further back, to the Ephesian converts of Saint Paul, who made bonfires of books they considered superstitious (books, I note with a bibliophile's eye, valued at "fifty thousand pieces of silver"), but the *Index* was the most consistent and longest-lasting censorship effort in Western civilization, and some years after its death it deserves a memorial, if only to salute such diligent and well-intentioned folly.

Folly it was. The final edition of the *Index* featured some four thousand works, many of them deservedly obscure and banned for doctrinal reasons, but many of them some of the greatest prose compositions in history: Michel de Montaigne's *Essais,* Gustave Flaubert's *Madame Bovary,* Victor Hugo's *Les Miserables,* the travel books of Laurence Sterne and Joseph Addison, John Milton's *State Papers,* Daniel Defoe's *History of the Devil,* Edward Gibbon's immense and wonderful *Decline and Fall of the Roman Empire,* and the complete works of Emile Zola, Thomas

Hobbes, and David Hume, among others. Some of these, like Addison's *Remarks on Several Parts of Italy,* were banned because of their irreverent portrayal of the Vatican City; others, like Montaigne's essays – from which the modern essay genre takes its form and spirit – were banned because of their dangerous relativism and individualism.

The *Index* did not begin in a purely condemnatory vein. Its first incarnation had three parts: a list of the authentic books of Scripture, a list of recommended readings, and a list of heretical and apocryphal books that the faithful were forbidden to study. The *Index* was a resounding success in its first millennium, since printing hadn't been invented and keeping an eye on the few books in the world wasn't difficult. Gutenberg's neat idea threw the Church into a tizzy, though, and in 1467 Pope Innocent VIII decreed that all new books had to be reviewed by authorities before general issuance. Thus came into being a phrase familiar, perhaps, to many readers: *imprimatur,* "it may be printed," the permission granted by the local authority, usually a bishop.

The *Index,* with many other aspects of ancient Catholicism, died at the hands of Catholicism's revolutionary Second Vatican Council, and it cannot be said that it is mourned by many, even among the most conservative Christians. One may admire, at this remove, its paternal intent to protect readers from "immorality"; but one may also excoriate its restriction of freedom, its anti-intellectual stance and tone, and its employment of an enduring evil, censorship, as a tool to encourage faith, which is the search for love amid evil.

A vibrant, dense, joyous faith of any stripe is one that punctures immorality and bad theology, not flees from it, or locks it away in cages. Evil is beaten not by retreat but by battle; and one of the most powerful tools readers and writers have against evils of all sort, including censorious religious monoliths, is their affection and respect for the word.

Rest in peace, *Index Librorum Prohibitorum,* for we are glad to see you gone and do not wish you well.

four

A Saint for Hardworking Women

We turn to *The Lives of the Saints* for many reasons, but one of the most human is to see what saint is honored on our own birthday – or, in other words, what saint we are especially to emulate. This morning, paging through the blizzard of saints and their vast and dramatic lives, we come to Saint Bertille, who is honored on November 6, and so we visit this good French nun, and look closely at her life in the monastery.

"Her prudence was so perfect that though she was still young, the care of entertaining strangers, and the charge of the sick and of the children that were educated in the monastery, were successfully committed to her," says the *Lives,* in its peculiarly ornate rhythmic parade of sentences. And up comes a picture of Bertille in our mind, bustling through the stone halls of the monastery at Jouarre, arranging meals for visitors, negotiating the purchase of medicine and bandages for the sick, hiring and training and supervising teachers, and all this before she was thirty years old, a mere child acting as public relations director, operations manager, maître d', and superintendent of education.

Soon enough she was promoted to abbess (at Chelles), and her monastery grew so famous as to lure "several foreign princesses and two queens" into it as nuns, but we prefer to keep not the renowned elder but the obscure younger Bertille in mind, for the busy young nun seems the more saintly to us. There are, and have always been, so many young women working so hard and so well, caring for the sick, arranging meals, managing the lives in and of their houses, educating children. Such precious work, so astonishingly important, so bereft of renown – but work with its own saint, for whom a prayer this busy morning.

As Strong As
the Very Ribs of the Earth

Among the many virtues of *The Lives of the Saints* is that it is consistently *revelatory;* no matter how many times one leafs through the terse accounts of those "friends, apostles, martyrs, co-heirs, brothers, and extraordinary benefactors," as they were called during the Second Vatican Council, one finds astonishing tales and people. Often their stories are like poems: short, magical, powerful lines that stay in the mind long after the book is closed and restored to its shelf.

The women of May, for example: Saint Jutta (May 5), Blessed Giselle (May 7), Saint Solange (May 10), Saint Dymphna (May 15), Saint Rita of Cascia (May 22), Saint Mary Magdalen de Pazzi (May 25), and closing the month with a bang, Saint Joan of Arc (May 30) and the Virgin Mary herself (May 31), on the feast day commemorating her visit to her cousin Elizabeth. Eight very different women (nine if we count Elizabeth) to be remembered during the month that we honor mothers and women. Who were these saintly women?

Jutta, patroness of Prussia, married at fifteen, widowed young, bringing up her children alone, so imbuing them with the faith that they all entered religious life; Giselle, married to Saint Stephen of Hungary and widowed young too, bringing up her son Saint Emeric alone; the French teenager Solange, shepherdess and healer, murdered by a nobleman who could not force his lust upon her; the Irish teenager Dymphna, patroness of the mentally ill, who refused her unstable father's wish to marry her, and so was murdered by him; the Italian Rita, patroness of impossible cases, whose husband beat her fiercely, but whose patient faith converted him on his deathbed; the Italian Carmelite nun Mary de Pazzi, prophetess and virgin; the famous Joan, who heard the voices of Saints Michael and Margaret and Catherine as a child in Lorraine, who commanded an army at the age of seventeen, who beat the English armies like drums, who was burned at nineteen; and the patient, mysterious, gentle Mary, who "proceeded in haste" to visit Elizabeth when she heard that her "aged" cousin was pregnant. And Elizabeth herself, miraculously and mysteriously pregnant at an age when she thought her womb would never be filled, and pregnant, to boot, with one of the most interesting and prickly characters in the New Testament, the testy and ferociously honest John the Baptist, he of the "garment of camel's hair, and a leather belt about his waist, and his food was locusts and wild honey."

What thread winds through the disparate tales of these women? Their courage, persistence, patience, character, and will; in a word, their extraordinary *strength*. The women mentioned above lived so many hard lives, lived them so well, with such astonishing resilience. Think of Jutta and Giselle the days after their husbands' deaths, rising before dawn, tasting the cold knowledge of their solitude and responsibility like stones in their throats – but gritting their teeth and setting to work raising their children, as so many millions of lonely women have done and do now, some in the very town where you read these words. Think of Solange and Dymphna, furious and terrified, knowing that their struggles would almost certainly bring mortal blows upon them, but too angry and brave to give in to a furious man. Think of Rita, who spent her whole life ducking blows, nursing bruises, seeing her own blood on the floor, but harboring a love so assured that she forgave day after day, blow after blow — the sheer *courage* of that woman, of women like her today, is nearly impossible to imagine. And the courage of Joan, not even twenty years old as she stood amid the flames searing her life away, and the courage of the gentle Judean girl Mary, who summoned all her courage one night and said to her hard-working quiet husband, *I am with child, and you are not the father, for the Child is the very Lord of Stars. . . .*

For a moment this day, for many moments this May, let us gape in awe at the strength of women, and look upon their sinewy courage with respect and humility, as the Lord looked on his Mother, and still does. Like Him we are of women born, and to women must pay our first respect, and owe our first love, for they are as strong as the very ribs of the earth.

A Note About Saint Finbar

Autumn is when the rains begin in northwestern North America, when *Is baisteach ar fhuinneoig ina clagarnaigh / Gan sanas air o thitim oiche,* "the rain is a tattoo on the window / Unslackening since the fall of night," as the Irish poet Maire Mhac an tSaoi writes. And one of the feast days of early autumn commemorates the life and work of an Irish poet who spent much of his life working in the Irish rain, a gentle and thorough water not unlike that which falls on the Pacific Northwest and maketh the land green and the mud muddier.

He was Finbar, or Barry as his name has come to be anglicized, and he was a fascinating fellow. Born late in the sixth century to an artisan and a lady of the Irish royal court, he was baptized Lochan but "received the name Fionbarr," as the *Lives of the Saints* says so politely, from the monks of Kilmacahill, Kilkenny, where the boy was schooled. Fionbarr in Gaelic means "white head," so apparently the wee lad was being teased by his teachers for his towheadedness; and so a grade-school joke descends to us from Ireland fourteen centuries ago.

Sometime during or immediately after his schooling in Kilkenny, Finbar began to walk and talk, Christlike, across the southern reaches of the island, preaching the Gospel and founding churches left and right. There are many

stories of him during this period: that he visited Saint
David in Wales; that he and David journeyed together to
Rome; that Pope Gregory was so impressed with Finbar
that he wished to make him a bishop on the spot, but a
vision from the Lord forbade the honor, as the Lord
wished to elevate the young man to sainthood Himself.

Finbar's last years were spent first as a hermit in
Gouganebarra and then as founder of a monastery at the
mouth of the River Lee, near Lough Eirc, in a marsh called
Corcaghmer. By then his fame was such that candidates
for the monastic life came from all over Ireland, and soon
the monastery had grown, and then a town sprang up
around it, and the town became a city, and thus came Cork,
through which many hundreds of thousands of Irish men
and women would pass on their way to America in the
1800s, many of those emigrants settling in Oregon, and
some of the descendants of those emigrants men and
women reading the very pages of this book. So a moment
of prayer for the soul of little Lochan with the white hair,
may he rest in peace in the hand of the Lord.

From *The Diary of Saint Kevin of Glendalough*

March 17, Saint Patrick's Day. Unbe*liev*able event this morning: I take my usual walk out into the woods, find a clearing, kneel down, stretch out my arms in supplication and prayer to the Lord, and a *blackbird lands in my left hand and lays a clutch of eggs*. Moral dilemma for me; I detest blackbirds, rats of the woods, and a handful of warm blackbird eggs makes me queasy, but I am of course constrained by my vow to love life in all creatures great and small. Have no choice but to remain still with arm outstretched. I write this with my right hand, as night falls. Holy Mary, Mother of God, get these eggs away from me, amen.

March 18, Saint Cyril's Day. My arm is *killing* me. The blackbird spent all of today building a nest around the eggs, and now I am holding not only incipient birds but plant stems, grass, leaves, twigs, roots, and mud. There are four eggs. They're bluish-white, speckled and mottled, not unlovely. I can tell them apart by the slightly different pattern of speckles as well as by their arrangement in my hand, nicely reflecting the four holy directions. Believe me, I've had a *lot* of time to look at them. Am so thirsty I can barely spit, and at dusk today I was forced to answer the call of nature. Good thing I am on a slight rise, a kind of mossy hillock in this clearing.

March 19, Saint Joseph's Day. Rain. I drank my fill of fresh water from the hand of the Lord, and blessed Him for His kindness to me. Got drenched. Always wondered what birds do to protect their eggs in a drenching rain. Answer: huddle over eggs and get drenched. Felt friendly toward the bird today, the two of us as wet as puppies. First time I felt friendly; have been feeling murderous. Forgive me, Lord.

March 20, Saint Wulfran's Day. Wulfran, famed for virtue in spite of the seductions of the world. Wonder if he had to spend four days on his knees in the mud with a bird in his hand and his arm as heavy as a class in hermeneutics. Feeling murderous again today. Very nearly dropped bird, eggs, and all when seized by sneezing fit first thing in the morning. Am starving. Am also wondering where the hell the rest of the monks are. Doesn't anybody miss me? Boy, when I get back to the abbey I am going to make the dust fly. "You're our leader, Kevin," "You're our inspiration, Kevin," "We wouldn't be here without you, Kevin," bah.

March 21, Saint Nicholas of Flue's Day. Nicholas was a hermit, too, spent nineteen years without taking food or drink, lived only on the Eucharist. *Tell* me about it. Partly cloudy today, chance of rain late in the afternoon.

March 22, Saint Lea's Day. Spent her nights in constant prayer. Ditto. Bird and I spent hours staring at each other today. I love bird. Bright yellow eyes, iridescent blue-black sheen, delicate fingery feet. I *really* love bird. Considered reaching over suddenly with my right hand and grabbing bird and stuffing her whole in my mouth and crunching her little bones happily and spitting out only her beak and toenails, but refrained after great struggle. Near thing, though. Bird knew nothing of this, I think.

March 23, Saint Turibius's Day. "Willingly exposed himself to the steaming climate of Peru," say the chronicles. Hmph. Bird eyeing me suspiciously today.

March 24, Saint Catherine of Sweden. Persuaded her husband to join her in a perpetual vow of chastity, foregoing their lawful marital rights for the love of God. No comment.

March 25, The Annunciation. Hard day. Exhausted, sick, starving, my robe is soiled, my breath stinks, my hair is matted, the flies and mosquitoes are biting great chunks from me, my arms and legs are wooden, and I have this itch *right* in the middle of my back, you know that one place that you just *cannot* reach no matter what? I think I sprained my right shoulder going for it. To be honest, it's all I can do to go on. I can't go on. I must go on. What did Mary say after the angel told her the news, though? "Let it be done to me as you say. . . ."

March 26, Saint Margaret. "Possessed of good looks, wit, and merriment," say the chronicles, "and crushed to death under great weight." Story of old Kevin of Glendalough. Snow in the morning, just a flurry. Reached over and cupped right hand over eggs and bird like little roof. Stared with interest at my hand, which looks like leather that's been left out in the weather.

March 27, Saint Rupert, missionary. Eggs stirred today. Flame of hope in me: they'll hatch! Tried desperately to remember what I learned in old Brother Brian's science class. *Turdus merula,* the Irish blackbird, incubation of eggs twelve to fifteen days. Whew. Good old Brother Brian. Sorry now that I used to mutter "what *possible* difference could knowing about *Turdus merula* ever make?" I was a dolt.

March 28, Saint Guntramnus. They didn't hatch, the bastards. Spent the day staring at the eggs, trying to heat them with my eyes, no luck. Rained all day. Starting to wonder if Brother Brian was off a bit on incubation; my God, what if it's 112 to 115 days?

March 29, Saint Joseph of Arimathea. Had the guts to ask for Christ's body. I vaguely remember my body. Spent the day today flying through the woods. I am a hawk now.

March 30, Saint John Climacus. I am an egg. I am the egg man. Once there was a Kevin and then he went to the woods and he died and they found him years later his bones like the bones of trees in the moss.

March 31, Saint Benjamin, martyr. Eggs hatched! Wet ugly birds struggled out of shell! At noon, when the sun reached its zenith, I slowly let my hand down and lay the cup of their nest on the moss. Rose creakily to feet. Thought about kneeling to thank Lord for hatching four new *Turduses,* thought better of kneeling and holding arm out in supplication ever again, decided to stand and pray with arms rigidly by sides henceforth, did little jig, with hands safely by side, to get blood flowing again, and so invented Irish step dancing. Blessed birds, including mother bird, who still eyes me warily. Must remember that blackbirds can apparently read minds. Stumbled home through woods to abbey. Cannot *wait* to have chat with brother monks such things as taking *attendance,* and *search* parties, and general *respect* for saints. Drooled thinking of first meal. Decided against eggs.

The Announciation

(A small laborer's hut in Nazareth, in Galilee, some years ago. Early evening, mere moments before sundown. A young woman, *perhaps eighteen, sits on a bench outside, waiting for her betrothed to return from his labors. Poking its head out of the attached stable is an aged* donkey.)

young woman

Hail, favored one! he says. Favored one . . . whew.

donkey

(quietly) You have to tell him, you know.

young woman

Tell him what? That an angel popped in this afternoon? With what you might call interesting news? He'd take that *real* well. You've heard him roaring about the wine not being served in the right jar, for heaven's sake.

donkey

How can you not tell him? I mean, you know, soon it'll be . . . evident.

young woman

I could visit Elizabeth for a while. Like nine months. Or a hundred years.

donkey

You're not riding *me* to the hill country of Judah, sweetie.
We made that trip once, remember? I got a hernia.

young woman

You faked that hernia, my friend – yes, you did. You *never*
liked Elizabeth. You never liked any of my family. Why,
right from the . . .

donkey

Here he comes! *(retreats into darkness of shed)*

young woman

(in a furious whisper) Ass!

young man

Hail, my beloved.

young woman

Yah, hail. Listen, Joe, sit down for a moment.

young man

But I must discard my dusty robe and hie me to the bath.
Ah, your wish to have me near cheers my heart; I wish our
wedding day all the closer. But I must cleanse myself, and
then there are evening prayers to be said *(his voice fading as
he enters the house)* and then our repast, with the wine maybe
in the right jars for a change. . . .

young woman

(whispers) I'm *screwed*.

donkey

(re-emerging) I'm telling you, you just have to tell him
straight out. It's the only way.

(young woman *shudders.*)

donkey
You want I should tell him? I'll tell him.

young woman
(smiling) Boy, that would be fun. But no, no. I'll do it.

young man
(re-emerging) An evening from the hand of the Lord, is it not, my love? And a poor dumb beast to share it.

donkey
(in a furious whisper) Ass!

young woman
Joseph, an angel appeared to me today.

young man
Hello?

young woman
Gabriel was his name. I was greatly troubled.

young man
An *angel?*

donkey
(whispers) Poor dumb beast . . .

young woman
He told me I would conceive a son, and His name would be Jesus, Son of the Most High, and His kingdom would have no end . . .

(young man's *mouth works but no sound emerges)*

young woman

(in a finishing rush) . . . and I said how could this *be,* because
I am a virgin, as you and I know *all* too well, and I said that
I wasn't even *married* yet, and he said nothing is im*poss*ible
with God, and I said okay, because I didn't know what *else*
to say, I mean the guy was an *angel,* about eighteen cubits
high, and you weren't here, there was no one here but him
(pointing to the donkey) . . .

(young man *whips around to stare at* donkey *with deep sus-
picion)*

young woman
. . . and then he departed from me.

young man
Who? Him? *(glaring at* donkey)

young woman
The angel.

young man
(totally rattled) The angel.

young woman
(abashed now at having spilled it all) The angel.

young man
Jesus!

young woman
Yes, that's what he said.

young man
Who? *(eyeing donkey bitterly again)*

young woman

The angel.

young man

(his dam bursting finally) You faked that hernia, damn it!
(waving his fist at the donkey) Faked it! And left me to carry
all that stuff home over the damned hills of Judah! I hate
the hills of Judah!

young woman

Joe . . .

young man

Damn it all! An angel! A hernia!

young woman

Joe . . . the baby . . .

young man

And you're to have a baby, and *God's* the father?! I court
you and win your hand and survive that damned trip to the
damned hills of Judah to see your family and get their precious approval and then we wait and wait and it's all I can
do to keep my hands to myself and then *God* sneaks in on
me?! *(roaring now) Am I supposed to believe this?*

young woman

(calmly, with amazing grace) It's true.

young man

I need a miracle here. I need it big-time. C'mon, Big Fella.
Show me. Show me I'm supposed to stay cool, marry
Mary, bring up a boy who isn't mine. C'mon. Hit me.

donkey

(loudly, calmly, every syllable clean and crisp) Joseph, Son of David, do not be afraid to take Mary as your wife; for that which has been conceived in her is of the Holy Spirit. And she will bear a Son; and you shall call His name Jesus, for it is He who will save His people from their sins.

young woman

(equally calmly, loudly, clearly, finishing the donkey's lines) "Behold, the virgin shall be with child, and shall bear a Son, and they shall call His name Immanuel . . ."

young man

(in a barely audible whisper) . . . God–with–us. *(Stunned, he plops down on the bench next to his fiance, and sits there slack-jawed. young woman puts left arm around young man and reaches right arm over to donkey, who kisses her hand; at that instant the sun plops down below horizon, stage lights dim, and . . .)*

finis

5
five

Grace Notes

Thoughts on a rich and riveting subject — divine, physical, emotional, prayerful, incomprehensible, inexhaustible grace.

Is there a richer and stranger idea in the world than grace? Only love, grace's cousin, grace's summer pelt.

Etymology: *grace* is the English translation of the Latin *gratia,* itself a translation of the Greek *charis,* itself a translation of various Hebrew words meaning, collectively, love, compassion, fidelity — all used in context of these gifts being utterly free from God to God's creatures. There are no requisites for grace, no magnets for it, no special prayers to lure it. No guru, no method, no teacher, as the Irish genius Van Morrison sings.

You can be good, bad, or indifferent, and you are equally liable to have grace hit you in the eye. *Non enim gratia Dei erit ullo modo nisi gratuita fuerit omni modo,* "it will not be the grace of God in any way unless it has been gratuitous in every way," says old Augustine, the grace-obsessed Bishop of Hippo, Augustine who considered the whole revolution of his life to be the direct result of a shock of grace. Grace is uncontrollable, arbitrary to our senses, apparently unmerited. It's utterly free, ferociously strong, and about as mysterious a thing as you could imagine.

First rule of grace: grace rules.

Grace lifts, it brings to joy. And what, as we age, do we cherish and savor more than joy? Pleasure, power, fame, lust, money, they eventually lose their fastballs, or should: At our best and wisest we just want joy, and when we are filled with grace we see rich thick joy in the simplest of things. Joy everywhere.

Notice how many saints — whom we assume were and are crammed to the eyeballs with grace — are celebrated for their childlike simplicity, their capacity to sense divine joy in everything: the daily resurrection of light, the dustiest of sparrows.

The undulating grace of horizons and waterlines, of new countries looming up through the mist as the ship nears harbor. The graceful lines of land fleeing in every direction from where you stand in the furrowed field. The smooth sweet swelling grace of a woman with child, the muscular grace of a man's knotted back at work. The cheek of child, the shank of youth, the measured grace of the aged.

The thin brave knobby-kneed yellow sticks that prop up herons, my wife's elegant neck when she folds back her hair with that unconscious practiced female flip of fingers, the slow pained kneeling of an old woman in chapel. In the lope of an animal loping. In a tree leaping very slowly sunward. In a child's hilarity. In the endurance of sadness. In the shudder of calm after rage.

In the bone of the character of a priest who walks to his breakfast with blood on his shoes, the blood of a student who died in his arms in the night after a drunken wreck, the priest is a wreck himself this bright awful dawn, minutes after he blessed the body, but he puts one foot in front of another and walks into a normal day because he is brave enough to keep living, and wise enough to know he has no choice, and he knows he received grace from the hand of the Lord when he needed it most, first when the boy terrified of dying grabbed him by the collar and begged to be told he would live forever and now, here, in the crack of a morning in a campus parking lot as he hesitates by his car, exhausted, rooted.

But he walks.

God grant me the grace of a normal day, prays my wife.

What would an alphabet of grace include? Acrobatic, blessed, calm, dignified, ecstatic, eternal, epiphanous, flowing, gentle, harmless, inexplicable, joyous, keen, lissome, momentous, near, oblique, opaque, peaceful, quiet, roomy, salvific, tireless, unbelievable, various, wondrous, xpeditious, yearning, zest.

Grace in the Old Testament is overwhelmingly a visual affair, from its first mention in Genesis, where Noah finds grace in the eyes of the Lord, to its last, when the Lord remarks to Zechariah that He will pour grace on the House of David, which will then be able to see "Me whom they have pierced" – an evocative foretelling of the Christ. Grace is "found in the eyes of the Lord," "found in thy sight," "found in your eyes," until one sees that the ancient people's sense of grace was favor, and they were constantly checking to see if they were on the good side of the One Who May Not Be Named. A crowd of the most interesting characters in the Old Book asks anxiously after grace: Joseph and Moses, Gideon and the sons of Gad and the sons of Reuben, Ruth and Hannah, David and Joab, Ziba and Ezra.

Only in the Psalms and Proverbs does grace open up and become something poured into lips and into the body, something to be granted to the lowly: *Though He scoffs at the scoffers / Yet He gives grace to the afflicted. . . .*

In the New Testament the Christ is grace personified – "the grace of God was upon him," according to Luke, and He is "full of grace and truth," says John, who makes a clear distinction between the prophets and the Messiah: "the law was given by Moses, but grace and truth came by Jesus Christ." The Apostles in their Acts are infused and suffused (and confused) by grace granted them by God, and they thrash out into the country from Jerusalem, teaching and preaching and wrestling awkwardly with their newfound power. Those who were not patient are now patient; those who could not preach now "speak boldly in the Lord, which gave testimony unto the word of His grace"; those

who were shy and clumsy are now "granted signs and won-
ders to be done by their hands."

That most interesting man Paul has the most interesting
things to say about grace in the Acts. He wants to "testify
the gospel of the grace of God," he says to the Ephesians
in his last meeting with them, commending them finally
"to God, and to the word of his grace, which is able to
build you up, and to give you an inheritance among all
them which are sanctified." In one of his densest and most
eloquent essays, to the Romans, he notes that faith is the
avenue to grace, which saves the soul – "access by faith into
grace in hope of the glory of God," as he says. To the
Romans he also insists that grace is utterly gratuitous,
unearnable: "If by grace, not now by works: otherwise
grace is no more grace." He bares all to the Corinthians,
and tells them that "to keep me from exalting myself, there
was given me a thorn in the flesh, a messenger of Satan, to
buffet me," and "concerning this I three times entreated the
Lord that it might depart from me, and He said unto me,
*My grace is sufficient for thee, for My strength is made perfect in
weakness."*

Grace sufficient to the size of your despair, neither more
nor less grace than you need . . . !

"Unto every one of us is given grace according to the
measure of the gift," says Paul, mysteriously; "He resisteth
the proud, and giveth grace to the humble," says Peter,
unmysteriously.

The final line of the New Testament speaks of grace,
John ending the account of his visions on the island of
Patmos with a blessing that has come down familiarly to
our time, and many times been spoken over the bowed

heads of the faithful, in a thousand languages: "The grace of our Lord Jesus Christ be with you all, amen." Thus Scripture ends with grace on its lips.

Can grace be granted all men, all women, all faiths, all nations, whether or not they have the word of God in their mouths and hearts? O yes o yes, the Church says — interestingly, has always said, no controversies and wrestling matches and murders done over the issue — a miracle. And it has eloquently said it, here and there. Orosius, one of Augustine's many disciples, said that grace was showered upon us all *quotidie per tempora, per dies, per momenta, cunctis et singulis* — daily through the seasons, through the days, through the moments, to all of us, to every one of us.

Each person experiences grace as he or she experiences human and divine love — which is to say, idiosyncratically, in ways different from all others. So we are all writing essays about grace all the time, in all sorts of languages.

Physical grace: a certain easy carriage, an authority of lightness, a liquid quickness or liability to litheness, a disciplined exuberance of the body, an unself-conscious ease, a comfortable residence in the body and world. All cats and women have it. Nearly all vegetative things. Most children, most animals, most trees. Many men. Generally the larger the entity the less grace; this is why we are agog at grace in the largest athletes and animals; why some people watch professional football; why circuses employ elephants, to wow the populace not with size so much as with unexpected grace in the gargantuan.

I think maybe we are so absorbed and attracted by physical grace because we sense how fleeting it can be, how very many enemies it has.

Graceful creatures: A pine marten racing fast and sure over talus and scree; my wife floating through a road race in a summer by a river; one of my sons, twisting in the air as he falls backward from a porch step, landing on his hands and knees and bouncing up again in a single smooth motion and sailing away at top speed, not a cry, not a scratch, my mouth falling open to see a body so quick to sense and react, so blindingly quick to rearrange itself. A body wholly at home in the ocean of quick.

"I have always been so sure I was right, that I was being led by God," wrote grace-riveted Dorothy Day (whose mother's name was Grace) in her middle years. "I confidently expected Him to show His will by external events. I looked for some big happening, some unmistakable sign. I disregarded all the little signs. I begin now to see them and with such clearness that I have to beg not to be shown too much, for fear I cannot bear it."

One of the few projects she never finished – she was a ferociously energetic woman, flinty, stubborn, not at all sweet, a perhaps-saint made of bone and glower – was a small book to be called *All Is Grace*. "The title really means 'all things work together for good to those who love God,'" she wrote.

Her favorite saint was another flinty woman obsessed by grace, Catherine of Siena, twenty-fourth of twenty-five children, a woman who received the (Dominican) habit at eighteen and then retired to her room for three years, coming out only for Mass. When she *did* emerge finally she was a dynamo, so respected by the Church that Pope Gregory XI granted her the power to absolve those who confessed sins to her. Catherine had visions during which God spoke to her at great length, and God, it turned out, is as grace-obsessed as Catherine and Augustine and Thomas and us: "My mercy is incomparably greater than all the sins anyone could commit," God said to Catherine. "This is that sin which is never forgiven, now or ever: the refusal, the scorning, of my mercy. For this offends me more than all the other sins they have committed. So the despair of Judas displeased me more and was a greater insult to my Son than his betrayal had been. My providence will never fail those who want to receive it."

Grace unfailable, inexhaustible, endless.

Oceans of grace, fountains of grace, rivers of grace. Water is an apt metaphor for grace; it is such a graceful creature itself, sinuous and ungraspable, the first ingredient of life, the substance that composes, cleanses, rejuvenates us, the sea in which we swam before birth.

The idea of grace winds thoroughly through religions. In Judaism, one earns grace: "Holiness is twofold," says the Kabbalah, "at first it is effort, then a gift. If you strive to be holy, you are eventually endowed with holiness. Be persistent in learning how to sanctify what you do. In the end, the Blessed Holy One will guide you on the path that it wishes and impart holiness to you, so that you become holy." In Hinduism, "make every act an offering to me [God]; regard me as your only protector," says the Bhagavad-Gita. "Remembering me, you shall overcome all difficulties through my grace." In Islam, "knowledge is possible for creatures via participation in Divine Knowledge, such participation being divine aid to creatures," says the Wisdom of the Prophets.

There are three fundamental themes in the Christian sense of grace, says the Jesuit theologian Roger Haight: It's "absolutely gratuitous," it is (as those rough saints Paul and Augustine discovered) "healing and sanative," and it's elevating. This last rivets me.

Further parse the language of apparitions for hints of the nature of grace. "I pour out a whole ocean of graces upon those souls who approach the fount of mercy on this day [the Sunday after Easter, the Feast of Divine Mercy] . . . on that day are open all the divine floodgates through which graces flow," said Jesus to a Polish girl in 1933, according to the diary of the girl, Helen Kowalska, later Blessed Sister Faustina, who coughed herself to death at age thirty-three.

Grace, says Augustine, is the only value in life and the truest presage of divine presence.

Many graceless arguments about grace over the centuries: The Thomists insisting that not Christ but the Trinity is the cause of grace in the angels and Adam and Eve. The Scotists insisting that all grace is from Christ. Pelagius and Augustine arguing about grace and free will – Pelagius, the fan of free will, losing and being bounced from the Church, banned for life, ineligible for the Hall of Fame. We grin now at the fussy ancient theologians splitting the ends of dry hairs about subjects forever beyond their ken and ours, but people were beheaded over these arguments, dismembered, disemboweled, exiled, impoverished, ruined. Later came the Inquisition, later came the military and economic wars in which people were sliced apart in incredible numbers, all ostensibly in the name of God, a bloody habit that the Church supported on and off over the centuries. Every Catholic at some point sighs for the Church in which we live, such a wonderful and cruel entity, such a brilliant and idiotic and lurching-gracelessly-toward-grace-enterprise.

I remember the words of Paul to the Corinthians: "The letter kills, but the spirit gives life."

Karl Rahner's final words on this earth, uttered, it is said, with startling authority and joy from a man minutes from morte: *All is grace!*

Another graceful ending: the great British preacher and writer Msgr. Ronald Knox. Drifting in and out of consciousness, Knox wakes to find a friend by his bedside. The friend asks if Knox would like to have some of the New Testament read to him – an edition that Knox has himself translated from the Greek.

"No," says Knox faintly.

And a few minutes later, even fainter:

"Awfully jolly of you to suggest it, though" – his last words.

God loves some of us violently; perhaps that savage love is a form of grace too. To wrench from you every shred of peace and feed you nothing but struggle sandwiches every day of your life – is that the highest form of Love? If you have the worst life imaginable and struggle ferociously against it, could it be that your fuel to fight is grace? Or that the measure of courage against your lot is the mark of your character?

How else to understand raped children, broken and bloodied and murdered children, children with ancient eyes, children who were never children, children who bear the marks of evil to their graves, children torn by evil as I write, as you read? *How else to understand them?* Tell me why they suffered and died, or suffered and did not die but were haunted and twisted all their lives by evil done upon them. Tell me why there have been so many millions of little broken Christs. Tell me.

And no one will tell me, for no one knows, only the inscrutable Lord, who never shows His hole cards. So I wonder if most grace in the world is spoken for by those who need it most, and those the smallest among us, their pain the greatest sin of our age.

Not-grace: disgrace, graceless. I listen to and read of people telling of the moments when they felt grace arriving and they use words like *calm, serene, harmony, peace, symmetry.* So grace flows, and the lack of grace — not-grace — is a damming of flow, jamming of gears, a stick in the spokes.

The only saint named for grace: Gratia, a fifteenth-century Dalmatian sailor who one day wanders into a Venetian church and is stunned by the sermon (from an Augustinian). Gratia joins the order and is sent to a monastery where he becomes a legendary gardener, and miracles of light and water follow him like puppies until the day he dies.

When have I been filled with grace? One time above all others, when my son was under ether. He was born with a broken heart, an incomplete heart, part of a heart. Not enough to keep him alive. Twice doctors cut him open and cut into his heart. Twice I waited and raged and chewed my fingers until they bled on the floor. Twice I sat in dark rooms with my wife and friends and savagely ate my skin.

The first operation was terrifying but it happened so fast and was so necessary and was so soon after the day he was born with a twin brother that we all mother father sister families friends staggered through the days and nights too tired and frightened to do anything but lurch into the next hour.

But by the second operation my son was nearly two years old, a stubborn funny amiable boy with a crooked gunslinger's grin, and when a doctor carried him down the hall, his moon-boy face grinning at me as it receded toward awful pain and possible death, I went somewhere dark that frightens me still. It was a cold black country that I hope never to see again. Yet out of the dark came my wife's hand like a hawk, and I believe, to this hour, that when she touched me I received pure grace. She woke me, saved me, not for the first time, not for the last.

As I finish writing these lines, I look up and my heart-healed son runs past the window, covered with mud and jelly.

❖

I grow utterly absorbed, as I age, by two things: love, thorough or insufficient, and grace under duress. Only those two. Politics, religion, money, ambition, they fade and are subsumed, consumed, eaten by these two vast and endless subjects: love and grace.

Those are the only things we will take to our graves, the only things that will be on our lips as we die, the only things that will be in our pockets as we walk to the country of the blessed – Tir na nOg it was called by my Irish people before me, the country of the always-young, where death has no dominion.

We love or do not love, we love well or badly, our friendships are a form of love, our enmities a form of not-love, missing love, weak love.

And grace under duress: what else is there?

Age and illness hammer us, tragedy and evil hammer us, greed and cupidity hammer us, we hammer ourselves in guilt and fear. What are we but the stories of how we fought against our troubles? What good do we remember of the dead but their humor, their stories, their courage, their selflessness, their grace?

"One day, I am invested mysteriously with my mother's grace," writes Louise Erdrich in *The Blue Jay's Dance,* a gentle and very honest memoir of the first year of her last child. "I am alone with our children. This has been a no-sleep week for each of them. At four in the morning of the fourth night I haven't slept, I sit down . . . weeping . . . and fall into a fifteen-minute coma before the next round begins.

"It happens to be a long crying bout, nothing wrong physically, just growth, maybe teeth. Who knows? Sometimes babies just cry . . . and cry. Morning drags in . . . our baby continues to cry. Then, in my office, with her in the crib next to the desk, I break through a level of sleep-deprived frustration so intense I think I'll burst, into a dimension of surprising calm.

"My hands reach down, trembling with anger, reach toward the needy child, but instead of roughly managing her they close gently as a whisper on her body. As though I am physically enlarged, I draw her to me, breathing deeply. The tension drops away. . . . I am invested . . . with my mother's patience. . . . Her hands have poured it into me. The hours she soothed me and . . . my younger brothers and sisters have passed invisibly into me. This gift has lain within me all my life, like a bird in a nest."

We think of grace arriving like an ambulance, just-in-time delivery, an invisible divine cavalry cresting a hill of troubles, a bolt of jazz from the glittering horn of the Creator, but maybe it lives in us and is activated by illness of the spirit. Maybe we're loaded with grace. Maybe we're stuffed with the stuff. Maybe it's stitched into our DNA, a fifth ingredient in the deoxyribonucleicacidic soup.

Grace at meals, that lovely habit of pausing to thank the Generosity who made the plants and fruits, the beasts of the earth and the birds of the sky and the fish of the sea — "even the *macaroni?*" says my daughter, and I say unto her Yea, even the macaroni, and also the Cheerios, and the cheese crackers, and the ginger snaps, for these foods have sustained her like no others, not even ye fruits and plants, of which she has cautiously partaken in nibbles that would mortify a mouse.

An ancient urge, the sigh of thanks at the prospect of food, and certainly a habit predating Christianity, but the peoples of the one God gave that whisper of relief and gratitude a graceful name, and made it a custom gentle and handsome.

Each home has its own grace or lack thereof, and the litany of formal and informal prayers at table is endless. As a boy I chanted a grace so old in our family that it often suffered hurried hungry editing into one long word — *BlessusOLordandthesethygiftswhichweareabouttoreceivefromthybountythroughChristOurLordAmen* — but as a man graced with small children, I ask them to name something for which they are thankful before we further reduce the macaroni population. *For my favorite shirt, for my basketball, for my ballet slippers,* they say grinning, but sometimes they say *for Mom,* or *for the air in my mouth,* and I think not for the first or last time that prayers from the smallest people are heard first.

Me, I am thankful for food. A moment ago in history my forebears ate dirt and grass and nothing in *An Gorta Mor,* the Hunger Great, the years when Irish children died so fast they littered the sides of the road and were stacked like wood in every corner of the country. I have never been hungry, and God grant that I never will; but there is something in me, some gnawing memory, that I think maybe is the shiver of old starving in my tribe – a shred of fear still hidden in the blood, a horror so strong that it stabbed past death into future generations. I notice that carelessly wasted food makes me so unreasonably angry that I frighten my children and myself when I roar at them over spills and splashes, over their petulant or reckless upsetting of bowls and plates. Their faces go pale and I have to leave the room and stand on the porch under cedars and pray for grace.

The greatest of grace scholars was Thomas Aquinas, a vast man in several senses – he was nicknamed the Dumb Ox as a student for his silence and bulk, and apparently was gifted with total recall of everything he had ever read, especially the Scriptures, which he committed to memory while imprisoned for two years. It was Thomas, in his massive *Summa Theologica*, who strove to explicate every intricate layer and corner of grace (*gratia actualis ad actum*, grace granted by God for the performance of salutary acts, disappearing when the act concludes; *gratia gratis datae*, the extraordinary grace granted miracle-workers, prophets, speakers in tongues, visionaries, priests, nuns, monks; *gratia illuminationis*, grace of the intellect; *gratia inspirationis*, grace of the will, etc.), and his treatise on the subject remains the primary scholarly tome. Three times in the last years of his life, Thomas was miraculously lifted into the air in church, and those present heard a voice from the crucifix say, *Thou hast written well of me, Thomas. . . .*

I ask a group of students from abroad about grace. *Grazia*, says an Italian girl, *nel senso spirituelle, nel senso fisico*, the same word carrying the double load it does in English. *Sancteiddrwydd*, says a young Welsh woman, or *truyaredd*, the latter more like mercy; physical grace would be simply *gras*. I tell them the Gaelic word for the name Grace: *Gráinne*, which hails from the oldest spoken Irish, and is thought to mean, rivetingly, She Who Strikes Fear.

Grace, says a French boy. *Eun-chong* in Korean, *milost* in Czech, *laun ch* in Chinese, *onchou* in Japanese, *ne'ama elaheiah* in Arabic, my head is spinning happily, the students cheerfully write or draw the word for me and try to explain how the idea feels in their languages, their countries, their hearts.

"Gracia," says a sweet shy Spanish girl. "It means the grace that God's catholic has. God has a power to protect and make full happy to people. It's a benediction of God. It's free."

The text of this book was typeset in Adobe Bembo. This typeface was produced by Monotype in 1929. The original alphabet type was designed for Petro Bembo's *De Aetna* in 1496 based on a roman cut by Francesco Griffo. *Credo* was set by MacLean and Tuminelly of Minneapolis, Minnesota, and printed on 60# Halopaque.

Genuine recycled paper with 10% post-consumer waste. Printed with soy-based ink.